POSTSCRIPT
LANGUAGE

TUTORIAL
and
COOKBOOK

POSTSCRIPT
LANGUAGE

TUTORIAL
and
COOKBOOK

ADOBE SYSTEMS
INCORPORATED

Addison-Wesley Publishing Company, Inc.

Reading, Massachusetts · Menlo Park, California · New York
Don Mills, Ontario · Wokingham, England · Amsterdam
Bonn · Sydney · Singapore · Tokyo · Madrid · San Juan

Library of Congress Cataloging in Publication Data

Main entry under title:

Postscript language tutorial and cookbook.

Includes index.
1. PostScript (Computer program language)
I. Adobe Systems.
QA76.73.P67P68 1985 005.13′3 85-15694
ISBN 0-201-10179-3
ISBN 0-201-10189-0

Fifth Printing, March 1989

EFGHIJ-HA-898

Contents

POSTSCRIPT LANGUAGE COOKBOOK

Preface

The POSTSCRIPT page description language provides a device independent standard for representing the printed page. This book is designed to be a companion piece to the *POSTSCRIPT Language Reference Manual*. It presents illustrative material to aid in understanding the POSTSCRIPT language. The tutorial information presented here has been deliberately separated from the reference manual to help ensure that the defining document offers a precise, unambiguous definition of the language and associated graphics imaging model. In all cases, when questions of definition or precise specification are raised, the *POSTSCRIPT Language Reference Manual* is the final word.

This book actually contains two documents: the *POSTSCRIPT Language Tutorial* and the *POSTSCRIPT Language Cookbook*.

The tutorial provides an easy, informal introduction to the POSTSCRIPT language and its graphics primitives. The tutorial's style and level of presentation is aimed at programmers who wish to design and implement applications, such as word processing packages, graphics illustrators, and CAD/CAM drawing systems. It is interactively oriented, and written with the assumption that you, the reader, already know how to program. You are encouraged to try variations of the examples presented in the tutorial on a POSTSCRIPT printer as you work your way through the book.

The cookbook is, as its name suggests, a collection of programs that are offered as examples of POSTSCRIPT usage. These samples have been chosen both as illustrations of the functional range of POSTSCRIPT and as useful ingredients for inclusion in application packages that you design. The cookbook samples demonstrate techniques for rendering quality graphics, achieving effective typography with digital fonts, and maintaining true device independence. Again, you are encouraged to experiment with variations of these samples on a POSTSCRIPT printer as you develop your own applications.

The principal authors of this material are Linda Gass and John Deubert. The final organization and the majority of the material for the *POSTSCRIPT Language Tutorial* is due to John Deubert. Ed Taft reviewed and proofread the material during the later stages of its production. Linda Gass designed and developed the *POSTSCRIPT Language Cookbook* and she is the principal author of both the examples and the explanatory text. The seminal idea of the cookbook is due to Doug Brotz and several of the illustrations in the cookbook are due to John Warnock. Andy Shore proofread the text and POSTSCRIPT sample programs. The book design was specified by Bob Ishi and was implemented by Andy Shore and Brian Reid. The index was compiled by Steven Sorensen.

The art of printing is rich in tradition, and the technology for producing the printed page has evolved over centuries. We at Adobe Systems are pleased to offer POSTSCRIPT as a tool for printing in the electronic age. I believe that this tutorial material will significantly enhance your ability to explore this exciting technology and help you enjoy the process of discovering the world of electronic printing.

Charles Geschke
August 1985

POSTSCRIPT
LANGUAGE

TUTORIAL

CHAPTER 1

INTRODUCTION

The POSTSCRIPT language is a programming language designed to convey a description of virtually any desired page to a printer. It possesses a wide range of graphic operators that may be combined in any manner. It contains variables and allows the combining of operators into more complex procedures and functions.

POSTSCRIPT page descriptions are programs to be run by an interpreter. POSTSCRIPT programs are usually generated by application programs running on other computers.

1.1 POSTSCRIPT AS A PAGE DESCRIPTION LANGUAGE

POSTSCRIPT has a large selection of graphics operators that allow it to precisely describe a desired page. These operators control the placement of three types of graphics objects:

- **Text** in a wide variety of typefaces can be placed on a page in any position, orientation, and scale.

- **Geometric figures** can be constructed using POSTSCRIPT graphics operators. These describe the locations of straight lines and curves of any size, orientation, and width, as well as filled spaces of any size, shape, and color.

- **Sampled Images** of digitized photographs, free-hand sketches, or any other image may be placed on a page in any scale or orientation.

All graphic objects may be easily rotated, scaled, and clipped to a specified portion of the output page.

POSTSCRIPT Imaging Model

An *imaging model* is the set of rules that are incorporated into the design of a graphics system. The POSTSCRIPT imaging model is very similar to the model we instinctively adopt when we draw by hand.

The POSTSCRIPT model considers an image to be built up by placing ink on a page in selected areas. The ink may form letters, lines, filled shapes, or halftone representations of photographs. The ink itself may be black, white, colored, or any shade of gray. These elements may be cropped to a boundary of any shape as they are placed on the page. Once the page has been built up to the desired form, it may be printed on an output device.

Three concepts are central to the implementation of the POSTSCRIPT imaging model:

Current Page: The *current page* is the "ideal page" on which POSTSCRIPT draws. It is independent of the capabilities of the printer being used.

When a program begins, the current page is completely empty. POSTSCRIPT *painting operators* place marks on the current page, each of which completely obscures marks that they may overlay. Once the current page is completely described, it is sent to the printer, which reproduces the page as well as it can.

It is important to remember that no matter what color a mark has—white, gray, black, or color—it is put onto the current page as if it were applied with opaque paint.

Current Path: The *current path* is a set of connected and disconnected points, lines, and curves that together describe shapes and their positions. There is no restriction to the shapes that may be defined by the current path; they may be convex or concave, even self-intersecting. The elements of the current path are specified in terms of their positions on the current page. The resolution of the printer in use in no way constrains the definition of the path.

The current path is not itself a mark on the current page. POSTSCRIPT *path operators* define the current path, but do not mark the page. Once a path has been defined, it can be stroked onto the current page (resulting in a line drawn along the path), filled (yielding solid regions of ink), or used as a clipping boundary.

Clipping Path: The *current clipping path* is the boundary of the area that may be drawn upon. Initially, the clipping path matches the printer's default paper size. The clipping path may be changed to any size and shape desired. If an imaging operator tries to mark the current page outside of the current clipping path, only those parts of the mark that fall within the clipping path will actually be drawn onto the current page.

Coordinate Systems

Positions on a page are described as x and y pairs in a coordinate system imposed on the page.

Every output device has a built-in coordinate system by which it addresses points on a page. We call this built-in coordinate system, idiosyncratic to each device, *device space*. Device space varies widely from printer to printer; there is no uniformity in the placement of coordinate origins or in horizontal and vertical scaling.

Positions on the POSTSCRIPT current page are described in terms of a *user coordinate system* or *user space*. This coordinate system is independent of the printer's device space. Coordinates in a POSTSCRIPT program are automatically transformed from user space into the printer's device space before printing the current page. User space thus provides a coordinate system within which a page may be described without regard for the particular machine on which the page is to be printed.

The POSTSCRIPT user space can be altered in three ways. The coordinate system's origin may be *translated*, moved to any point in user space. The axes may be *rotated* to any orientation. The axes may be *scaled* to any degree desired; the scaling may be different in the x and y directions. A sophisticated user may specify any linear transformation from user space to device space. Thus, coordinates in a POSTSCRIPT program are changeable with respect to the current page, since they are described from within a coordinate system that may slide around, turn, shrink, or expand.

1.2 POSTSCRIPT AS A PROGRAMMING LANGUAGE

About one-third of the POSTSCRIPT language is devoted to graphics. The remainder makes up an entirely general computer programming language. The POSTSCRIPT language contains elements of many other programming languages, but most closely resembles the FORTH language.

POSTSCRIPT Stack

POSTSCRIPT reserves a piece of memory called a *stack* for the data with which it is working. The stack behaves like a stack of books. The last book placed on the stack is the first book that will later be removed. Similarly, numbers, strings, and other pieces of data placed on the stack will be removed in reverse order, the last item added to the stack being the first retrieved.

Postfix Notation

POSTSCRIPT operators that require numbers or other data, such as **add** and **sub**, retrieve that data from the stack. To use an operator, one must first place the data it requires, its *operands*, on the stack, and then call the operator. The operator will place its own results on the stack. This style of programming, in which the operands are specified before the operator, is referred to as *postfix notation*.

POSTSCRIPT Data Types

POSTSCRIPT supports many data types common to other languages, including reals, booleans, arrays, and strings. The POSTSCRIPT language also defines object types such as *dictionary* and *mark*. For descriptions of all the POSTSCRIPT data and object types, refer to the *POSTSCRIPT Language Reference Manual*.

POSTSCRIPT Flexibility

POSTSCRIPT is an extremely *flexible* language. Functions that do not exist, but which would be useful for an application, can be defined and then used like other POSTSCRIPT operators. Thus, POSTSCRIPT is not a fixed tool within whose limits an application must be written, but is an environment that can be changed to match the task at hand. Pieces of one page description can be used to compose other, more complicated pages. Such pieces can be used in their original form or translated, rotated, and scaled to form a myriad of new composite pages.

Printable Programs

POSTSCRIPT programs are written entirely in printable ASCII characters. This allows them to be handled as ordinary text files by the vast majority of communication and computer file systems. In addition, it ensures that a POSTSCRIPT program will be as easy for a person to read as the structure of the program allows.

CHAPTER 2

STACK AND ARITHMETIC

The POSTSCRIPT programming language, like all programming languages, works with various types of data, such as numbers, arrays, strings, and characters. The pieces of data manipulated by POSTSCRIPT are referred to as POSTSCRIPT *objects*.

There are many ways a language can manipulate data; for example, many languages require that data be placed in variables and be addressed by a variable name. The POSTSCRIPT language has variables, but it also manipulates data directly by using a special entity called a *stack*.

2.1 THE POSTSCRIPT STACK

A stack is a piece of memory set aside for data which is to be immediately used by POSTSCRIPT. This memory area is organized in such a way that the last item put in is the first item available to be removed. This type of data structure is referred to as a *last in, first out* or *LIFO* stack.

A LIFO stack behaves like a stack of books. As the books are stacked up—Twain, then Dickens, then Hemingway, and so on—only the book on the top, the last one added, is really accessible.

Putting Numbers on the Stack

Any number appearing in a POSTSCRIPT source file (that is, a text file that contains a POSTSCRIPT program) is placed on the stack. For example, if a source file contains the following line:

12 6.3 −99

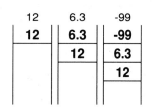

POSTSCRIPT Stack

the interpreter will take the following actions as it reads the line from left to right (see illustration at left):

1. Push the number *12* onto the stack

2. Place *6.3* on the stack, pushing *12* to the next position down.

3. Put *−99* onto the stack, pushing the first two numbers down one place.

The number *−99* is now at the top of the stack, waiting to be used. The other numbers are on the stack also, but can only be taken off in the proper order. It should be borne in mind as we use the stack that *any* kind of POSTSCRIPT object can be placed on the stack. This includes arrays, strings, and the more exotic POSTSCRIPT objects, like dictionaries. For the first chapter or two of this tutorial, we shall concentrate primarily on numbers, to simplify our discussion.

Anything can be placed
on the stack

Note that spaces, tabs, and newline characters act as delimiters of POSTSCRIPT objects. Other characters, such as parentheses and brackets, can be delimiters under some circumstances; we shall discuss these as we progress through the tutorial.

2.2 ARITHMETIC

A POSTSCRIPT *operator* is a word that causes the POSTSCRIPT interpreter to carry out some action. It is the equivalent of the commands and procedures of other languages. When the interpreter comes across a word in a source file, it searches its internal dictionaries to see if that word is an operator name. If the name is listed in the dictionary, the interpreter carries out whatever instructions are associated with that name and then continues on to the next word in the source file. For more detail on POSTSCRIPT dictionaries, refer to chapter four.

add and sub

POSTSCRIPT operators look to the stack for the numbers they need, that is, for their *operands*. The operator generally removes its operands from the stack and replaces them with whatever results that operator produces.

For example, the **add** operator causes POSTSCRIPT to remove the top two numbers from the stack, add them, and leave the sum on the stack. Thus, the program line below would affect the stack as illustrated at left.

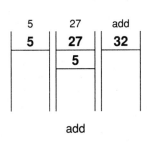

add

> 5 27 add

The *5* and the *27* are pushed onto the stack and the **add** operator then replaces them with their sum.

The POSTSCRIPT **sub** operator works in a similar manner, with the program line

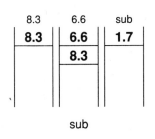

sub

> 8.3 6.6 sub

having the results diagrammed at left. The numbers *8.3* and *6.6* are pushed on the stack; the **sub** operator subtracts the top number on the stack from the number below it.

Stack Notation

The contents of the POSTSCRIPT stack is typically depicted in print as a line of numbers (or other data) with the top of the stack at right. Thus, a stack with *6* on top, *143.9* below it, and *−800* below that is printed:

> −800 143.9 6

Notice that this displays the numbers in the order in which they were originally placed on the stack.

Similarly, the effects of an operator on the stack may be indicated by showing the stack's initial condition (before the operator is executed), the operator's name, and then the contents of the stack after the operator was executed. Using this method, a demonstration of the effects of **add** could be expressed:

$$5\ 27\ \textbf{add} \Rightarrow 32$$

Other Arithmetic Operators

Besides **add** and **sub**, POSTSCRIPT possesses a full range of arithmetic operators, including:

div   Divide the second number on the stack by the top number on the stack. For example,

$$13\ 8\ \textbf{div} \Rightarrow 1.625$$

idiv   Divide the second number on the stack by the top number on the stack; only the integral part of the quotient is retained.

$$25\ 3\ \textbf{idiv} \Rightarrow 8$$

mod   Divide the second number by the top. In this case, only the remainder of the division is kept.

$$12\ 10\ \textbf{mod} \Rightarrow 2$$

The operands passed to the **mod** and **idiv** operators must be integers.

mul   Multiply the top two numbers on the stack, pushing the product onto the stack.

$$6\ 8\ \textbf{mul} \Rightarrow 48$$

neg   Reverse the sign of the number on top of the stack.

$$-27\ \textbf{neg} \Rightarrow 27$$

These are the arithmetic operators we shall be using the most in this tutorial. For detailed descriptions of the full range of POSTSCRIPT arithmetic operators, including **sqrt**, **exp**, **ceiling**, and **sin**, see the *POSTSCRIPT Language Reference Manual*.

More-Complex Arithmetic

The use of a stack in POSTSCRIPT allows some freedom in exactly how an arithmetic process is carried out. For example, let us say that we wanted to calculate

$$6 + (3 \div 8)$$

in POSTSCRIPT. Either of the following two program lines would leave the appropriate number on the stack.

- 3 8 div 6 add

- 6 3 8 div add

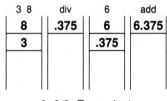

6+3/8, Example 1

In the first case (see illustration), we put *3* and *8* on the stack, divide the former by the latter, put *6* on the stack, and add it to the quotient below it.

In the second case, the same operations are performed, but now we start out by putting all three of the numbers on the stack. Then we call the **div** operator, which divides the second number (*3*) by the top (*8*) and add the top two numbers (*6* and *.375*).

6+3/8, Example 2

Similarly, the equation

$$8 - (7 \times 3)$$

can be expressed in at least two ways:

- 8 7 3 mul sub

- 7 3 mul 8 exch sub

The second method introduces a new operator: **exch**. This operator exchanges the top two items on the stack. Note that in this example, the phrase *7 3 mul* places the two numbers on the stack and multiplies them, leaving the product, *21*, on the top of the stack. The number *8* is then pushed onto the stack, but this leaves the stack contents in the wrong order for our subtraction. The **sub** operator subtracts the top number from the second, which in this case would be *21* minus *8*, the opposite of what we want. The **exch** operator invoked at this point reverses the order of the top two numbers of the stack, putting them in the correct order for our subtraction.

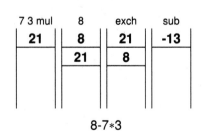

8-7*3

Stack Operators

The **exch** operator is our first example of a *stack operator*, an operator whose function is to add, remove, or rearrange items on the POSTSCRIPT stack. There are several such operators, including:

clear   Removes all items from the stack.

        6 8 12 **clear** $\Rightarrow$ —

dup   Duplicates the top item on the stack.

        6 **dup** $\Rightarrow$ 6 6

pop   Remove the the top element from the stack.

        17 8 **pop** $\Rightarrow$ 17

roll   Roll stack contents. Take two numbers from the stack. The top number tells POSTSCRIPT how many times and in which direction to rotate the stack; the second number is how many items are to be rotated.

        7 8 9 3 1 **roll** $\Rightarrow$ 9 7 8

        7 8 9 3 –1 **roll** $\Rightarrow$ 8 9 7

We will be using these and other stack manipulation operators throughout this manual. For a complete description of all these operators, see the appropriate chapter in the *POSTSCRIPT Language Reference Manual*.

2.3 INTERACTIVE STACK OPERATORS

Most POSTSCRIPT programs are generated by application programs such as word processors. However, many POSTSCRIPT printers have an interactive mode that allows a user to speak directly to the POSTSCRIPT interpreter. For those who do have an interactive environment, POSTSCRIPT has operators that allow you to directly examine the stack.

==

15.3	-17
-17	98
98	

(a)　　(b)

The == operator removes the top item from the stack and echos it over a communications channel (which is often connected to a terminal). Thus, if the stack looked like figure *a*, at left, the == operator, typed on the keyboard, would print *15.3* on the terminal and leave the stack holding the contents indicated in *b*.

The == operator prints the top item as well as it can. Many objects, such as numbers, strings, and arrays, are simply printed. Items that cannot be printed, like dictionaries and files, are identified by their object types. Thus, if the top item on the stack was a dictionary (we shall be talking about this at greater length later), the == operator would print

　　—dictionary—

on the terminal.

pstack

Another useful interactive stack operator is **pstack**. This operator prints the contents of the entire stack. Unlike the == operator, **pstack** does not remove any of the stack's contents.

Thus, if the stack looked like this:

　　6 12 –97.2 100

The **pstack** operator would display the following, leaving the stack unchanged.

　　100
　　–97.2
　　12
　　6

pstack and == are examples of *polymorphic operators*, so called because they can take many different kinds of objects as operands.

2.4 NEW OPERATOR SUMMARIES

This chapter, and those that follow, end with a summary of the POSTSCRIPT operators introduced in the chapter. These summaries group the new operators by function type and list the following information for each:

- Operator name
- Stack contents before operation
- Stack contents after operation
- Description of operation

The two lists of stack contents are separated by a double arrow ($\Rightarrow$). The symbols used in the stack descriptions represent the following types of objects:

n i j x y	Numbers
ary	Array
bool	Boolean
dict	Dictionary
fdict	Font dictionary
nam	Name
ob	Any POSTSCRIPT object
proc	Procedure
str	String

Other symbols, when used, are self-explanatory. When more than one type of object may be expected on the stack, the alternative types will be separated by a slash (/). Thus, *ary/str* indicates that the object may be either an array or a string.

2.5 OPERATOR SUMMARY

Stack Operators

clear $ob_1...ob_i \Rightarrow$ —
Remove all stack contents

dup $ob \Rightarrow ob\ ob$
Duplicate top of stack

exch $ob_1\ ob_2 \Rightarrow ob_2\ ob_1$
Reverse order of top two objects on stack

pop $ob_1\ ob_2 \Rightarrow ob_1$
Remove top of stack

roll $ob_{n-1}...ob_0\ n\ j \Rightarrow ob_{(j-1)\ mod\ n}...ob_0\ ob_{n-1}...ob_{j\ mod\ n}$
Rotate n elements j times

Math Operators

add $n_1\ n_2 \Rightarrow n_1 + n_2$
Add two numbers

div $n_1\ n_2 \Rightarrow n_1 \div n_2$
Divide two numbers

idiv $n_1\ n_2 \Rightarrow int(n_1 \div n_2)$
Integer divide

mod $n_1\ n_2 \Rightarrow (n_1\ MOD\ n_2)$
Modulus

mul $n_1\ n_2 \Rightarrow n_1 \times n_2$
Multiply two numbers

sub $n_1\ n_2 \Rightarrow n_1 - n_2$
Subtract two numbers

Interactive Operators

== $ob \Rightarrow$ —
Destructively display top of stack

pstack $ob_1...ob_i \Rightarrow ob_1...ob_i$
Display stack contents

CHAPTER 3

BEGINNING GRAPHICS

The POSTSCRIPT language is designed to produce graphic images. This being the case, the language comes with a wealth of graphics operators, which we shall be exploring in this tutorial.

Drawing with POSTSCRIPT starts with constructing a *path* on an ideal drawing surface called the *current page*. A *path* is a set of straight lines and curves that define a region to be filled or represent a trajectory that is to be drawn on the current page. (For a more complete discussion of paths and the current page, refer to the *POSTSCRIPT Language Reference Manual.*)

Having constructed a path, we need to decide what to do with it. We can paint a line of some thickness along the current path or we can fill the path in to create a solid shape.

We will alternate these two steps—creating a path and filling or stroking it—until everything we want has been drawn onto the current page. Once the current page is complete, we can print it on a physical piece of paper.

3.1 DRAWING LINES

Let us begin with a simple task: drawing a single 5-inch-long vertical line. The following program accomplishes this.

```
newpath
  144 72 moveto
  144 432 lineto
stroke
showpage
```

Let us examine this program line by line.

We start out by calling the **newpath** operator. This operator empties the current path and declares we are starting a new path.

Now we shall construct a straight path that corresponds to the line we wish to draw. Paths are constructed by moving a phantom "pen" around the current page. This pen leaves an unmarked trace on the current page that represents the current path. The position on the current page to which this pen points at a particular time is the *current point* on the current path.

We start building a path with a **moveto**.

```
144 72 moveto
```

The **moveto** operator takes two numbers off the stack and treats them as x and y coordinates to which to move. The coordinates specified become the current point.

In the POSTSCRIPT default coordinate system, the origin is in the lower left hand corner of the current page. As usual, x increases to the right and y increases upward. The units employed in this system are 1/72 inch long. Thus, our second program line places two numbers (*144* and *72*) on the stack and then moves the current point to a location 2 inches (144/72) to the right and 1 inch (72/72) up from the lower-left corner of the page.

The **lineto** operator on the third line,

```
144 432 lineto
```

adds a segment to the current path that connects the current point to the position specified by the numbers on the stack, in this case *144* and *432*. The point specified as the argument to this operator becomes the new current point.

Note that the **lineto** operator does not actually draw on the current page. It simply adds a line segment to the current path. You may later draw in this line, but it does not happen automatically.

The **stroke** operator on line four causes the path we have constructed to be painted onto the current page. Our path becomes a visible line.

Finally, **showpage** prints the current page, with the line we drew on it.

The three steps we took in drawing our line were:

1. Construct a POSTSCRIPT path, using **newpath**, **moveto**, and **lineto**.

2. **stroke** that path onto the current page.

3. Print the current page with **showpage**.

Two Lines

The following program, whose output is at left, draws two lines.

```
newpath
  72 360 moveto
  144 72 rlineto
  144 432 moveto
  0 –216 rlineto
stroke
showpage
```

This program is similar to our first. The first two lines clear the current path and move the current point to a position 1 inch to the right and 5 inches up from the page's lower-left corner.

```
newpath
  72 360 moveto
```

The next line contains a new operator, **rlineto**.

```
144 72 rlineto
```

This is similar to the **lineto** operator we used in the first program. Here, however, the numbers on the stack represent an x and y displacement relative to the current point. POSTSCRIPT also has an **rmoveto** operator that is similar to **moveto**, but measures positions relative to the current point.

Thus, the program line above adds a line segment to the current path. This segment extends two inches to the right of, and one inch above, the current point.

The next two lines of the program,

```
144 432 moveto
0 –216 rlineto
```

move the current point up above the first line segment and then add a line segment to our path extending *down* (note the negative y argument) *216* units from that point.

At this stage we have a path consisting of two intersecting line segments. These lines would be invisible if we were to print the current page right now, since we have not yet used the **stroke** operator. Note that the current path is not continuous. A POSTSCRIPT path does not need to be a single connected piece; it can consist of *any* collection of line segments and curves on the current page.

Finally, our program strokes the path and prints the current page.

A Box

Here's a simple one-inch-square box, centered on the page:

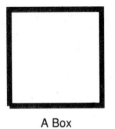

A Box

```
newpath
  270 360 moveto
  0 72 rlineto
  72 0 rlineto
  0 –72 rlineto
  –72 0 rlineto
  4 setlinewidth
stroke showpage
```

This program moves to a position near the center of the page and then constructs a box-shaped path by moving one inch up, right, down, and left. The path is then stroked and the page printed.

The seventh line presents something new:

    4 setlinewidth

The **setlinewidth** operator allows you to specify the width of the line that is stroked onto your path. In this case, a line width of 4/72 inch is specified; this will remain the width of all lines stroked onto the page until a new **setlinewidth** is invoked.

Our box, you may notice, contains a flaw: the lower-left corner has a notch in it. This results from our lines' having significant width.

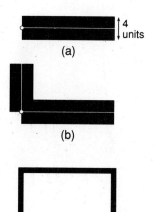

(a)

(b)

A four-unit-wide line segment extends two units to either side of the current path (illustration *a*, at left). Where the first and last line segments of our box intersect, there is a two-unit-square area that is not a part of either stroked path and remained white (illustration *b*).

To avoid this problem, we must use a new operator: **closepath**.

```
newpath
  270 360 moveto
  0 72 rlineto
  72 0 rlineto
  0 −72 rlineto
  closepath
  4 setlinewidth
stroke showpage
```

A Better Box

This program is identical to the previous one, save that the program line closing the box has been changed to **closepath**. The **closepath** operator adds a line segment to the current path connecting the current point to the last point addressed by a **moveto** operator. It closes the path with a mitered join, eliminating the notch we noticed in our first box. It is possible to change the method by which POSTSCRIPT joins line segments; to see how this is done, refer to chapter 9 of this tutorial.

3.2 FILLED SHAPES

Our programs so far have constructed paths and then stroked them onto the page. However, a POSTSCRIPT path can also be filled in. The following program is identical to the last except for one line.

A Filled Box

```
newpath
  270 360 moveto
  0 72 rlineto
  72 0 rlineto
  0 −72 rlineto
  closepath
  fill
showpage
```

This time, instead of stroking this path, we invoked the **fill** operator. This operator fills the current path with ink, producing a solid black square.

A Gray Box

Our block does not have to be black. The program below produces a gray box.

A Gray Box

```
newpath
  270 360 moveto
  0 72 rlineto
  72 0 rlineto
  0 −72 rlineto
  closepath
  .5 setgray
  fill
showpage
```

The **setgray** operator specifies the shade of gray in which all painting is to be done. The argument on the stack (0.5, in this case) specifies the shade, with zero being black and one being white. The gray shade specified will remain in effect until another **setgray** changes it. If a program does not specify a gray value, POSTSCRIPT assumes everything is to be painted in black.

Your printer may produce halftones that look different from those printed in this tutorial. Each printer has its own method of generating these.

Overlapping Shapes

POSTSCRIPT images are opaque. Any ink painted on the current page will obscure anything previously painted there. Consider this program, for example, which paints three overlapping solid squares.

Overlapping Boxes

```
newpath         %Begin black box
  252 324 moveto
  0 72 rlineto
  72 0 rlineto
  0 -72 rlineto
  closepath
  fill

newpath         %Begin gray box
  270 360 moveto
  0 72 rlineto
  72 0 rlineto
  0 -72 rlineto
  closepath
  .4 setgray
  fill

newpath         %Begin lighter box
  288 396 moveto
  0 72 rlineto
  72 0 rlineto
  0 -72 rlineto
  closepath
  .8 setgray
  fill
showpage        %Send to printer
```

This example paints a black box, an overlapping gray box, and an overlapping light gray box. Each box covers up part of the box below it. If we had painted a white box, that would also have covered up whatever it overlapped.

Note that each box had to start with a **moveto**. This is because the **fill** operator clears the current path; after a **fill**, there is no current point and a **lineto** or **rlineto** would have no starting point. The **stroke** operator also clears the current path.

The three-box program also contains comments. Comments in POSTSCRIPT programs start with a percent symbol and continue to the end of the line. Anything following a % on a POSTSCRIPT program line is ignored by the interpreter.

This last program was quite repetitious; we performed a set of operations—drawing a filled box—three times. We shall see in the next chapter that the POSTSCRIPT language allows you to define a group of operations as a named procedure. This procedure can then be used exactly as though it were a POSTSCRIPT predefined operator.

3.3 OPERATOR SUMMARY

Path Construction Operators

closepath — ⇒ —
Closes the current path with a straight line to the last *moveto* point

lineto x y ⇒ —
Continue the path with line to *(x,y)*

moveto x y ⇒ —
Set the current point to *(x,y)*

newpath — ⇒ —
Clear the current path

rlineto x y ⇒ —
Relative *lineto* (currentpoint + *(x,y)*)

rmoveto x y ⇒ —
Relative *moveto*

Painting Operators

fill — ⇒ —
Fill current path with the current color

setgray n ⇒ —
Set the current color

setlinewidth n ⇒ —
Set the current line width

stroke — ⇒ —
Paint the current path with the current color and line width

Output Operators

showpage — ⇒ —
Transfer the current page to the output device

CHAPTER 4

PROCEDURES AND VARIABLES

4.1 POSTSCRIPT DICTIONARIES

A dictionary is a table that associates pairs of objects. An English dictionary associates words with their definitions. A POSTSCRIPT dictionary associates an object called a *key* with another object, the key's *value*. The POSTSCRIPT interpreter can look up a key in a dictionary and obtain the associated value (or discover that the key is not present).

Two POSTSCRIPT dictionaries are always present, the *system dictionary* and the *user dictionary*. The system dictionary pairs each predefined POSTSCRIPT operator name with a particular built-in action. The POSTSCRIPT *user dictionary* associates names with the procedures and variables defined by a program.

When the interpreter encounters a name, it searches first the user dictionary and then the system dictionary. If it finds the name among the dictionaries' keys, the interpreter takes the appropriate action, usually either putting an object on the stack or carrying out a set of instructions. If the name is not found in the dictionaries, the interpreter raises an error.

POSTSCRIPT dictionaries are kept on a *dictionary stack*, which starts out with the system dictionary on the bottom and the user dictionary on top. When the interpreter encounters a name, it searches the dictionaries downward from the top of this stack. A program may create new dictionaries, which can be placed on top of the dictionary stack. The dictionary on top of the dictionary stack, and thus the first to be searched, is called the *current dictionary*. For details on creating new dictionaries, refer to the *POSTSCRIPT Language Reference Manual* and the *POSTSCRIPT Language Cookbook*.

4.2 DEFINING VARIABLES AND PROCEDURES

POSTSCRIPT Variables

A variable is defined by placing the variable's name and value into the current dictionary. This is done with the **def** operator, as in the following program line:

    /ppi 72 def

This line first places the name *ppi* onto the stack. The slash preceding these characters indicates that the POSTSCRIPT interpreter should put this name on the stack as a *literal* and not immediately try to find it in a dictionary.

Next, the number *72* is pushed onto the stack.

Finally, **def** takes these two objects off the stack and enters them into the current dictionary. The second item on the stack (*ppi*) becomes the key that is associated with the first item (*72*). That is, *ppi* is now a POSTSCRIPT variable with a value of *72*. If the line

    10 ppi mul

were to appear later in our program, the POSTSCRIPT interpreter would do the following:

1. Push *10* on the stack,

2. Search the dictionary stack for the key *ppi* and put its value, *72*, on the stack,

3. Multiply the top two stack items together, leaving their product on the stack.

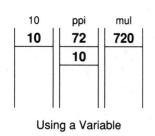

Using a Variable

To change the value of a variable, you redefine it with a new value. The following lines would both change the value of *ppi*.

    /ppi 100 def

    /ppi ppi 1 add def

The first line would redefine *ppi* to a value of *100*; the second would increment the value of *ppi* by one (see illustration at left).

/ppi	ppi	1	add
ppi	**100**	**1**	**101**
	ppi	**100**	**ppi**
		ppi	

Incrementing a Variable

POSTSCRIPT Procedures

A POSTSCRIPT procedure is a set of operations grouped together with a common name. This set of operations is stored with its key in a dictionary. When the key appears in a program, the associated set of operations is carried out.

POSTSCRIPT procedures are defined in exactly the same way as variables. The program must place the procedure name (preceded by a slash) on the stack, followed by the set of operations that make up the procedure. Then the **def** operator is used to store the operations and name in the current dictionary. The set of operations making up the procedure must be enclosed in braces.

For example, the following line defines a procedure named *inch*.

    /inch {72 mul} def

Any appearances of the word *inch* following this line will cause the interpreter to carry out the operations inside the braces. That is, the interpreter will put *72* on the stack and then multiply the top two numbers, the *72* and whatever was on the stack when *inch* was called. Thus, the program lines

    5 inch
    5 72 mul

have identical results; both leave *360*, the product of *5* and *72*, on the stack.

The *inch* procedure is a useful tool in many programs, since it translates inches into the 1/72-inch units of the POSTSCRIPT coordinate system.

4.3 USING PROCEDURES AND VARIABLES

The use of procedures and variables can make an enormous difference in the readability of a program, the ease with which it can be modified, and its length.

Three Boxes Again

As an example, let us take the last program from chapter two, the three overlapping boxes, and rewrite it. Looking over the program, we see that the set of instructions that construct a one-inch-square path is repeated three times. Let us define these instructions to be a procedure named *box* and then incorporate this procedure into the program.

Overlapping Boxes

```
% ----- Define box procedure ---
/box
  { 72 0 rlineto
    0 72 rlineto
    -72 0 rlineto
    closepath } def
% --------- Begin Program -----------
newpath           % First box
  252 324 moveto box
  0 setgray fill
newpath           % Second box
  270 360 moveto box
  .4 setgray fill
newpath           % Third box
  288 396 moveto box
  .8 setgray fill
showpage
```

Here we start by defining our new procedure, *box*, to be the set of operators that create a square path. We then use that procedure three times to make three filled boxes. First we move to a starting point on the current page. Then we call the *box* procedure, which contructs a path starting at that point. Finally, we set the gray value and fill the path we contructed. These steps are repeated two more times, once for each box in our image.

Advantages

Changing our program has affected it in three important ways:

1. The program is more compact.

2. The program is more readable. Procedure names can (and should) be chosen to reflect what they do. In reading the program later, you can more easily see what the program is doing at any given point, since the procedure titles themselves tell you.

3. The program is more easily changed. If, for example, we wanted it to create two-inch boxes, we would only need to change the definition of the *box* procedure. In the earlier version of this program, we would have had to separately change each of the three boxes.

Another Box Program

The way in which one designs a program will vary according to what decisions have been made in defining procedures. Let us look at one more way of producing our overlapping boxes.

```
% ------- Define procedures----
/inch  {72 mul} def

/box               % stack: x y => ---
{ newpath moveto
  1 inch 0 rlineto
  0 1 inch rlineto
  −1 inch 0 rlineto
  closepath } def

/fillbox            % stack: grayvalue => ---
{ setgray fill } def

% ----------- Main Program -----------
3.5 inch 4.5 inch box
0 fillbox
3.75 inch 5 inch box
.4 fillbox
4 inch 5.5 inch box
.8 fillbox
showpage
```

We have made three changes here. First of all, we have included our *inch* procedure, which converts the number on the stack from inches into POSTSCRIPT units.

Second, we changed *box* so that it clears the current path (**newpath**) and then moves to the location specified on the stack before tracing out its path. Note that the comment to the right of the procedure name indentifies what the procedure expects to find on the stack.

Finally, we defined *fillbox*, which sets the current gray value to the number on the stack, and then **fill**s the current path.

This new version of our program divides into two sections. We first defined a set of procedures and then used these procedures in the main part of our program, the section that actually carries out our assigned task. This main program section is much more readable than our original three-box program. Units are expressed in inches and major activities are carried out by procedures whose names indicate their functions.

Considerations in Defining Procedures

There are no solid rules that dictate when a set of operations should be defined as a procedure. In general, the three qualities you are trying to maximize are: *readability*, so that other people (or yourself at a later date) can pick up the program and see what it does; *compactness*, so that your program does not take up more space than is necessary; *flexibility*, so that when changes become necessary, they can be made with a minimum of pain.

To maximize these qualities, you should consider defining a set of operations to be a procedure if it occurs frequently in the program, particularly if it is likely to need revising, or if its purpose is obscure to the casual reader and would benefit from a descriptive name.

4.4 OPERATOR SUMMARY

Dictionary Operators

def   key value $\Rightarrow$ —
Associate *key* with *value* in the current dictionary

CHAPTER 5

PRINTING TEXT

A great deal of what we put on paper is text in various forms. The POSTSCRIPT language has all the tools necessary to handle text operations, from simple word placement to complex typographic composition.

Text data is represented by POSTSCRIPT *string* objects. A POSTSCRIPT string consists of any sequence of characters enclosed in parentheses. A string can be placed on the stack, assigned to a variable, or printed on paper.

POSTSCRIPT allows considerable freedom in how a string is printed. Before a string can be sent to the current page, POSTSCRIPT must be told what typeface and size to use in the printing. That is, you must specify the *font*.

5.1 POSTSCRIPT FONTS

A *font* is a collection of characters with a unified design. The design itself is referred to as a *typeface*. A set of typefaces designed to work together in a pleasing way is called a *typeface family*.

There are hundreds of typeface families, including such familiar ones as Times and Helvetica.

Roman
Italic
Bold
Extended
Condensed
Obliqued

The typefaces within each family represent variations on the theme set by the family's design. Thus, within the Times family, we have Times Roman, Times Italic, Times Bold, and so on. The variety of possible faces within a family is endless and includes typefaces that are extended, condensed, extra-bold, and obliqued.

A font is a particular implementation of a typeface. The standard POSTSCRIPT fonts are geometrical descriptions of the outlines of a typeface's characters. These descriptions allow the font to be printed on paper at any scale with minimum distortion from the scaling process.

Using POSTSCRIPT Fonts

Before you can print text, you must specify the desired font. There are three steps to this process:

1. Find the information describing the font. This information is kept in a *font dictionary*, which contains the information necessary to produce a particular font, including the outline description of each character. For more information on font dictionaries, refer to chapter eight of this tutorial and to the *POSTSCRIPT Language Reference Manual*.

2. Scale the font to the size needed. The size is specified by the minimum vertical separation necessary between lines of text. Thus, a twelve-point font needs twelve points between successive lines of text to ensure the lines do not interfere with each other. (Remember that a point is 1/72 inch.)

3. Establish the scaled font as the *current font*, in which all text is to be printed.

To see how this is done, let us examine the following program, which prints the word *typography* in 15-point Times Roman.

typography

```
/Times-Roman findfont
15 scalefont
setfont
72 200 moveto
(typography) show
showpage
```

There are several new operators here.

In the first line we put the literal name *Times-Roman* on the stack and then call the **findfont** operator.

/Times-Roman findfont

findfont looks up the name in a dictionary called **FontDirectory** and places the appropriate font dictionary on the stack.

The font dictionary returned by the **findfont** operator contains character shape descriptions for one-point characters. These must be changed to the desired font size with the **scalefont** operator. This operator takes a font dictionary and a number from the stack, and returns the font dictionary scaled by the specified amount.

Thus, our program's second line

15 scalefont

will leave on the stack a dictionary for a 15-point Times Roman font.

Finally, the **setfont** operator takes the font dictionary off the stack and establishes it as the *current font*, to be used for printing text.

Now we are ready to print something.

We use the **moveto** operator to set the current point. Then we place the string *typography* on the stack (enclosed in parentheses to denote it as a string), and call the **show** operator.

72 200 moveto
(typography) show

show prints the string that is on the stack onto the current page starting at the current point. The current point is left at the end of the text.

5.2 PRINTING VARIETY

Point Sizes

The fact that POSTSCRIPT internally describes its fonts as shape descriptions allows the fonts to be scaled while retaining their fidelity at large sizes. For example, consider the following program:

Gorilla

Gorilla

Gorilla

Gorilla

```
/showGorilla      % stack: x y ---
 { moveto (Gorilla) show }def
/Times-Roman findfont  6 scalefont  setfont
72 300 showGorilla
/Times-Roman findfont  10 scalefont  setfont
72 275  showGorilla
/Times-Roman findfont  15 scalefont  setfont
72 250  showGorilla
/Times-Roman findfont  20 scalefont  setfont
72 225 showGorilla

showpage
```

This program prints the word *Gorilla* in four different sizes of Times Roman. We first define a procedure called *showGorilla*, which moves to a position specified on the stack and then prints the string.

```
/showGorilla      % stack: x y ---
 { moveto (Gorilla) show }def
```

The procedure is followed by a set of lines that repeatedly finds, scales, and sets a Times Roman font and then calls *showGorilla*.

```
/Times-Roman findfont  6 scalefont  setfont
72 300 showGorilla
```

Note that this program could also be written with a procedure defined to handle the font changes:

```
/showGorilla      % stack: x y
 { moveto (Gorilla) show }def

/scaleTimes      % stack: scale
 { /Times-Roman findfont
   exch scalefont                    %scale, using # on stk
   setfont } def

6 scaleTimes
72 300 showGorilla
10 scaleTimes
72 275  showGorilla
15 scaleTimes
72 250  showGorilla
25 scaleTimes
72 225 showGorilla

showpage
```

The *scaleTimes* procedure defined above sets the current font to Times Roman at a point size obtained from the stack. The first line of the *scaleTimes* definition retrieves the font dictionary for Times Roman.

```
/Times-Roman findfont
```

The stack now has this dictionary on top and the scale we want below it. (We placed the font dictionary on the stack when we called the procedure.) We exchange these two objects and call the **scalefont** and **setfont** operators.

```
exch scalefont
setfont
```

The current font becomes Times Roman at the desired point size.

Typefaces

The following program demonstrates the POSTSCRIPT standard typefaces.

```
%-------- Define Procedures ------------
/vpos  720 def  % vertical position variable
/word  (Typefaces) def          % string variable

/choosefont      % Stack: typeface-name
{ findfont 15 scalefont setfont} def

/newline
{/vpos vpos 15 sub def          %decrease vpos
 72 vpos moveto } def           %go to that line

/printword        %stk: typeface-name
{ choosefont      %set font
  word show       %show "typefaces"
  newline } def   %go to next line

%------------ Begin Program ----------------
72 vpos moveto %vpos starts as 720
/Times-Roman    printword
/Times-Bold    printword
/Times-Italic    printword
/Times-BoldItalic  printword
newline
/Helvetica    printword
/Helvetica-Bold  printword
/Helvetica-Oblique  printword
/Helvetica-BoldOblique  printword
newline
/Courier    printword
/Courier-Bold  printword
/Courier-Oblique  printword
/Courier-BoldOblique  printword
newline
/Symbol    printword
showpage
```

Typefaces
Typefaces
Typefaces
Typefaces

Typefaces
Typefaces
Typefaces
Typefaces

`Typefaces`
`Typefaces`
`Typefaces`
`Typefaces`

Τψπεφαχεσ

This program is more elaborate than our earlier ones. We start by defining two variables and three procedures.

The variable *vpos* is used to keep track of the current point's vertical position. The program uses this variable as the *y* argument of a **moveto**.

Word holds the string that we want our program to print. It will be used by a **show** operator.

The *choosefont* procedure

```
/choosefont      % Stack: typeface-name
{ findfont 15 scalefont setfont} def
```

sets the current font to that named on the stack. *Newline* moves the current point down fifteen points by decreasing *vpos* and using it with a **moveto**.

```
/newline
{/vpos vpos 15 sub def
 72 vpos moveto } def
```

The *printword* procedure sets the current font, using *choosefont*, prints the value of the variable *word*, and then moves the current point to the beginning of the next line, using *newline*.

```
/printword       %stk: typeface-name
{ choosefont
  word show
  newline } def
```

After defining its variables and procedures, the program moves the current point to a starting position on the current page and then uses *printword* with nine different typefaces.

```
/Times-Roman   printword
/Times-Bold    printword
/Times-Italic   printword
/Times-BoldItalic  printword
newline
```

Note that the typeface families are separated by calls to the **newline** procedure.

Graphics and Text

POSTSCRIPT makes no distinction between text and graphics. A text character is simply another graphic object to be placed on the current page. Thus, no special steps need to be taken to combine text and graphics on an output page.

Let us end this chapter with an example that illustrates this point. We shall design and print a business card for the world-famous *Diamond Cafe*.

This will be a standard-size business card (two inches by three-and-a-half) and will have a printed border 1/8 inch in from the card's edges. We shall print the name of the cafe in bold type at the top left of the card with the cafe's slogan ("The Club of Lonely Hearts") in italics below it. In the lower-right corner will be the name of the cafe's owner. Behind the text, we shall print a light gray diamond.

```
%---------------- Variables -----------------
/MainFont
    /Helvetica-Bold findfont 15 scalefont def
/SloganFont
    /Helvetica-Oblique findfont 7 scalefont def
/OwnerFont
    /Helvetica findfont 10 scalefont def

%---------------- Procedures ------------------
/rightshow        % stk: string
  { dup stringwidth pop          %get length of string
    120 exch sub %calc. white space
    0 rmoveto       %Move over that much
    show } def      %show string
```

```
/CardOutline     %Print card's outline
 { newpath
   90 90 moveto
   0 144 rlineto
   252 0 rlineto
   0 –144 rlineto
   closepath
   .5 setlinewidth
   stroke } def

/doBorder        %Print card's border
 { 99 99 moveto
   0 126 rlineto   %Border: 126 pts high
   234 0 rlineto   %  & 234 points wide
   0 –126 rlineto
   closepath
   2 setlinewidth %2-point-wide line
   stroke } def

/Diamond
 { newpath        %define & fill
   207 216  moveto              % a diamond-shaped
    36 –54  rlineto             % path
   –36 –54  rlineto
   –36  54  rlineto
   closepath
   .8 setgray  fill } def

/doText          %Print card's text
 { 0 setgray  90 180 moveto
   MainFont setfont
   (Diamond Cafe) rightshow
   90 168 moveto
   SloganFont setfont
   ("The Club of Lonely Hearts") rightshow
   216 126 moveto
   OwnerFont setfont
   (Sam Spade) show
   216 111 moveto
   (Owner) show } def
```

```
%---------- Main Program ------------
CardOutline
doBorder
Diamond
doText

showpage
```

This program defines several variables and procedures and then uses them to make the card. The steps taken in printing the card are suggested by the procedure calls at the end of the program. The card's outline is drawn, followed by the border, the gray diamond, and the text.

Any POSTSCRIPT object can be assigned to a variable. This program uses three variables whose values are font dictionaries. Each of these variables holds the information needed to reproduce characters in a particular font. All the program needs to do to change fonts is place the value of the desired variable on the stack and call the **setfont** operator.

Let's examine the definition of the *MainFont*. We first place the name of the variable on the stack as a literal, preceded by a slash:

```
/MainFont
```

We then put the font dictionary for the Helvetica Bold typeface on the stack

```
/Helvetica-Bold findfont
```

and scale it to a point size of fifteen.

```
15 scalefont
```

The **scalefont** operator leaves the newly-scaled font dictionary on top of the stack with our variable name still residing beneath it. The **def** operator places these two objects into the user dictionary, with *MainFont* as the key and the font dictionary as that key's value.

```
/MainFont
    /Helvetica-Bold findfont 15 scalefont def
```

The other two variables, *SloganFont* and *OwnerFont* are similarly defined.

Assigning scaled font dictionaries to variables is a good practice in programs that frequently change fonts. Finding and scaling a font dictionary is a relatively time-consuming task. If a program does this once for each font and saves the result as a variable, it will run much more quickly than if it calls the **findfont** and **scalefont** operators for each font change.

Five procedures are defined in this program.

Rightshow prints a right-justified string (taken from the stack) in a 120-point-wide space. The first line of this procedure's definition

```
dup stringwidth pop
```

introduces a new operator: **stringwidth**.

stringwidth takes a string from the top of the stack and replaces it with the horizontal and vertical distances the current point would be moved if the string were shown in the current font. The *y* offset is left on top of the stack, with *x* below it. Thus, the line above duplicates the string on the stack, replaces the top copy of the string with the *x* and *y* offsets, and then drops the *y* offset from the stack. The stack is left with the string's width on top of the stack and the string itself below.

The procedures *CardOutline*, *doBorder*, and *Diamond* all define closed paths. *CardOutline* and *doBorder* stroke their paths onto the current page, while *Diamond* fills its path with gray.

Finally, *doText* prints the card's lettering in a succession of **moveto**s, **setfont**s, and *rightshow*s. Note that the different fonts are set by calling one of the font-dictionary variables and then **setfont**.

5.3 OPERATOR SUMMARY

Character and Font Operators

findfont   key $\Rightarrow$ fdict
Return dictionary for named font

scalefont   fdict n $\Rightarrow$ fdict
Return new scaled font dictionary

setfont   fdict $\Rightarrow$ —
Set current font

show   str $\Rightarrow$ —
Print *str* on the current page

stringwidth   str $\Rightarrow$ x y
Return width of *str*

CHAPTER 6

MORE GRAPHICS

6.1 COORDINATE SYSTEMS

POSTSCRIPT graphics operators do their work within a coordinate system refered to as the *user coordinate system* or *user space*. This system is independent of any physical device; POSTSCRIPT operators draw in user space and the result is automatically transferred to the *device coordinate system* of a particular printer, that is, to *device space*.

In our programs so far, we have been using the POSTSCRIPT default coordinate system. In this *default user space*, the origin is in the lower-left-hand corner of the current page and the unit of measure is the POSTSCRIPT unit of 1/72 inch.

User space is malleable, however. Its coordinate system may be changed in position, orientation, and size.

Translating User Space

Translation is movement from one place to another. In the case of a coordinate system, it refers to movement of the origin. The POSTSCRIPT **translate** operator moves the origin of user space to the position specified on the stack. For example, the program line

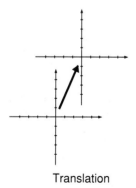

Translation

100 200 translate

would move the origin of the POSTSCRIPT coordinate system to the point *(100,200)*. All future positions will be measured from this point on the current page.

The following program illustrates the effects of **translate**.

```
/Times-Roman findfont 30 scalefont setfont

/square          %procedure to draw a
 { newpath       %  filled square
   0 0 moveto
   90 0 lineto    %define a square path
   90 90 lineto
   0 90 lineto
   closepath  fill %fill it
   6 92 moveto   % & label it
   (A Box) show  } def

square           %do a square
200 250 translate              %move coord. sys.
square           %do another square
200 250 translate              %and move again
square           %do a third square

showpage
```

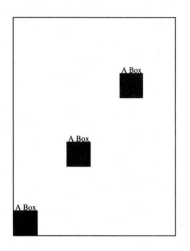

Translated Squares

The procedure defined in this program draws a block whose lower left corner is at the origin of the current coordinate system. We obtained three different blocks in this program, not by changing the position of each box, but by translating the origin of the coordinate system on the current page. Note that the second translation was relative to the already-once-translated origin, not the default origin.

Thus, there are two ways of drawing an object in several places. You can change the position of the object each time, substituting new coordinates where necessary, or you can construct the object at the same coordinates and move the coordinate system.

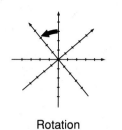

Rotation

Rotation

The POSTSCRIPT user coordinate system may also be rotated. The **rotate** operator takes a number from the stack and rotates the coordinate axes that many degrees counterclockwise.

Let us again write a program that draws a box three times, translated as before, but this time also rotated.

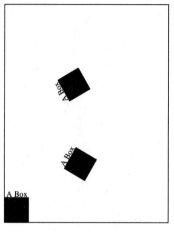

Rotated Squares

```
/Times-Roman findfont 30 scalefont setfont

/square              %procedure from
 { newpath           % previous program
  0 0 moveto
  90 0 lineto
  90 90 lineto
  0 90 lineto
  closepath  fill
  6 92 moveto   %Label the box
  (A Box) show } def

square              %do a square
300 150 translate                %move coord. sys.
60 rotate           %and rotate it
square              %do it again...
300 150 translate
60 rotate
square              %do a third square

showpage
```

Again, we changed the position and orientation of the square by changing the coordinate system within which that square is defined. The actual definition of the square is unchanged.

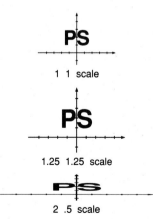

1 1 scale

1.25 1.25 scale

2 .5 scale

Scaling

The **scale** operator allows you to change the size of the units used by POSTSCRIPT. This operator takes two arguments from the stack, an x and y scaling factor, and changes the size of the coordinate system's units by those factors. For example,

3 3 scale

will triple the size of the coordinate system's units; objects will be drawn three times as large as they would have been before this command was executed.

Again, our box program:

```
/Times-Roman findfont 30 scalefont setfont

/square          %procedure to draw a
 { newpath       % filled square
  0 0 moveto
  90 0 lineto
  90 90 lineto
  0 90 lineto
  closepath  fill
  6 92 moveto   %Label the box
  (A Box) show  } def

square           %do a square
100 100 translate
1.5 1.5 scale
square
100 100 translate
.75 1.25 scale    %non-uniform scaling
square

showpage
```

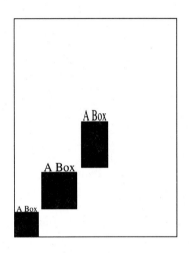

Scaled Squares

Notice that the second scaling was *non-uniform*; we scaled the *x* and *y* dimensions by different factors, making our square (and its label) appear narrow and tall.

6.2 GRAPHICS STATE

In our programs so far, we have been implicitly working within a *graphics state*, the set of data that describes how POSTSCRIPT operators will affect the current page. Among the information that makes up the current graphics state are the current *path*, *point*, *gray value*, *font*, *line width*, and *user coordinate system*.

For a complete description of the graphics state, refer to the *POSTSCRIPT Language Reference Manual*.

Saving the Graphics State

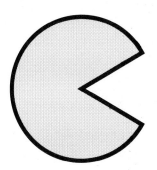

There are times when we would like to save the current graphics state so that we can return to it at a later time.

For example, if we want to print a filled and outlined shape, such as the one at left, we would have to construct a suitable path and then fill it. Unfortunately, the **fill** operator clears the current path, leaving us with no path to stroke. It would be useful to save the current graphics state immediately before performing the **fill** and then restore the graphics state afterwards, recovering the path which could then be stroked.

The operators that save and retrieve the current graphics state are **gsave** and **grestore**. The **gsave** operator saves a copy of the current graphics state on a *graphics state stack*. This stack can hold up to thirty-two graphics states, including the current graphics state.

The **grestore** operator restores the most recently gsaved graphics state. All of the characteristics of the current graphics state, including the current path, gray value, line width, and user coordinate system, are returned to what they were when the **gsave** operator was called.

Let us demonstrate the use of these operators with a program that draws a five-pointed star, filled and outlined.

```
/starside
{ 72 0 lineto      %add line to path
  currentpoint translate        %move origin
  −144 rotate } def             %rotate coord. sys.

/star             %stack: x y
{ moveto
  currentpoint translate
  4 {starside} repeat
  closepath
  gsave
    .5 setgray fill
  grestore
  stroke } def
```

Star

200 200 star

showpage

We have defined two procedures in this program. *Starside* draws one of the lines that make up the star; *star* draws a filled, outlined star whose upper left point has the *x* and *y* coordinates specified on the stack.

The *starside* procedure starts out by adding a horizontal line to the current path:

72 0 lineto

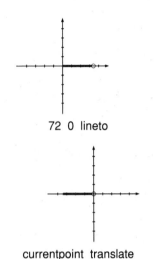

72 0 lineto

It then introduces a new operator, **currentpoint**, which pushes the *x* and *y* coordinates of the current point on the stack. The program line

currentpoint translate

currentpoint translate

thus puts the coordinates of the current point on the stack and then moves the origin of user space to that position. The origin is moved to the end of the line segment we just added to our path.

The *starside* procedure then rotates the current coordinate system 144 degrees clockwise.

−144 rotate

(Note the negative argument; positive angles are measured counterclockwise.) This rotation reorients the *x*-axis in the direction of the next side of the star.

-144 rotate

The *star* procedure also introduces a new operator, **repeat**.

4 {starside} repeat

This operator requires two arguments: a number (*4*, in this case) and a set of operations enclosed in curly braces (here consisting of the procedure *starside*). The operations are carried out the number of times specified by the first operand. The line above will thus perform the *starside* procedure four times.

This line is followed by a **closepath**, which completes the star-shaped path.

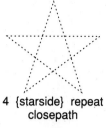

4 {starside} repeat
closepath

fill

grestore

stroke

We then fill in the star:

```
gsave
  .5 setgray fill
grestore
```

Before we fill the star, we use the **gsave** operator to copy the current state on the graphics state stack. This is necessary because we want to use the current path twice: once to **fill** and once to **stroke**. Having saved the graphics state, we set the gray level to .5 and **fill** the path. **fill** clears the current path. When we call **grestore**, the graphics state we duplicated earlier is restored as our current graphics state, returning the star-shaped path and a gray value of *0*.

The *star* procedure then strokes the resurrected current path.

The main part of our program is only two lines long:

```
200 200 star
```

```
showpage
```

This pushes *200* on the stack twice (as *x* and *y* coordinates) and calls the *star* procedure, constructing a star beginning at that point. The **showpage** operator then commits the contents of the current page to paper.

6.3 CURVES

Generally, graphic images are not composed exclusively of straight line segments. To accomodate this, there are POSTSCRIPT operators to construct any desired curve. In this section, we shall discuss curves that are circular arcs. More complex curves may be defined using such operators as **curveto** (see the *POSTSCRIPT Language Reference Manual*).

The **arc** operator adds a circular arc to the current path. It requires five arguments on the stack: the *x* and *y* coordinates of the arc's center of curvature, the *radius* of curvature, and the arc's beginning and ending *angles* measured counterclockwise from the positive *x* axis. Thus, the program line

100 150 36 45 90 arc

would produce an arc-shaped path on the current page with a center 100 units to the right and 150 units above the origin, a radius of 36 units, extending counterclockwise from 45 to 90 degrees (see illustration at left).

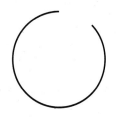

100 150 36 45 90 arc

The **arcn** operator is similar to **arc**, differing only in that it constructs an arc in a clockwise direction. The line

100 150 36 45 90 arcn

produces a path shaped like that at left.

100 150 36 45 90 arcn

The **arc** and **arcn** operators alter their behaviors slightly if a current point already exists when the operator is called. In this case, the operator will draw not only the specified arc, but also a line segment connecting the current point and the beginning of the arc.

The following program illustrates this change by drawing similar arcs, first without and then with a current point.

```
newpath
300  400  54  40  140  arc  stroke

newpath
300 365 moveto
340  345  54  40  140  arc  stroke

showpage
```

Two arcs

In the first case, no current point exists; the arc is simply drawn onto the current page as specifed. Before drawing the second arc, however, we moved the current point to the position *340,365*; this time, the **arc** operator drew a line connecting our current point to the beginning of the arc.

Circles and Ellipses

A circle is an arc extending from 0 to 360 degrees. An ellipse can be constructed by nonuniformly scaling the coordinate system and then drawing a circle.

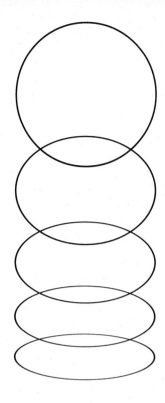

Ellipses

The program below draws a series of ellipses.

```
/doACircle
 { 0 0 54 0 360 arc stroke } def

/doAnEllipse
 { 1 .75 scale
   doACircle
   stroke } def

300 500 translate  doACircle

4 {0 −72 translate
   doAnEllipse} repeat

showpage
```

We begin by defining two procedures, *doACircle*, which draws a circle 54 units in radius with its center at the origin, and *doAnEllipse*, which draws an ellipse by scaling the *y*-dimension to three-quarters the *x* and then drawing a circle.

The program translates the origin to a position above the middle of the page and draws a circle. Then the program does the following operations four times, using a **repeat** operator:

1. Move the coordinate origin down one inch (72 units).

2. Draw an ellipse onto the current page.

Note that although our loop specifies a one-inch distance between the ellipses' centers, the ellipses are not drawn one inch apart. This is because they are offset 72 points as measured in the current coordinate system, whose y-direction is scaled down by each ellipse.

Note also that although we only specify a scaling factor of .75, the y axis becomes scaled much more than this during the program. Each ellipse scales the *current* coordinate system, which may already be scaled. Each ellipse reduces the vertical direction to three-quarters of what it was before.

Rounding Corners

Intersecting lines are frequently connected by round corners. The POSTSCRIPT **arcto** operator offers a convenient way to do this.

The operator requires two points and a radius on the stack. It draws a line segment from the current point toward the first point listed on the stack. This segment terminates in an arc with the specified radius whose end is tangent to the line segment connecting the two points specified on the stack (see illustration at left). The operator returns with the stack holding the x and y coordinates of the beginning and end of the arc.

This becomes much clearer with an example. The following program draws a small x at each of three points, moves to the first of these, and then uses the other two points as arguments to **arcto**.

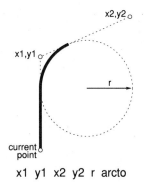

x1 y1 x2 y2 r arcto

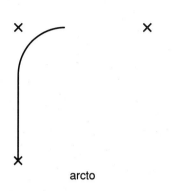

arcto

```
/DrawAnX
  { 3  3  rmoveto  –6  –6  rlineto
    0  6  rmoveto  6  –6  rlineto
    stroke } def

50 50 moveto DrawAnX
50 150 moveto DrawAnX
150 150 moveto  DrawAnX

50 50 moveto
50 150  150 150  36 arcto
4 {pop} repeat
stroke

showpage
```

The results of this program are shown at left. After drawing the three *X*'s, the program moves the current point to *50,50*, the lower left point. The **arcto** operator then starts drawing a line segment toward *50,150* (in the upper left). Instead of extending up to the point, the line segment ends with an arc of radius *36* that terminates tangent to the line connecting the top two points in the diagram. The current point is left at the end of the arc.

Note that the **arcto** operator leaves the stack holding the numbers *50, 114, 86,* and *150*, which represent the beginning and endpoint of the arc. Since we do not need these values, we drop them from the stack with a repeated **pop** operator.

```
4 {pop} repeat
```

Printing a Logo

Let us use our curve-generating operators to print a logo for a movie named *Omaha*. This movie dwells on the loneliness of the Plains during the early nineteenth century and so its logo will be rather stark, consisting of a black background with the word "Omaha" rising from below and a gray circle, representing the full moon, behind.

```
% ------------ Define Procedures -------------
/Helvetica-Bold findfont  27 scalefont setfont

/fourpops
{ 4 {pop} repeat } def

/background                        %Black background
{ 0 18 moveto                      % with rounded corners
   0 72  108 72  18 arcto fourpops
   108 72  108 0  18 arcto fourpops
   108 0  0 0  18 arcto fourpops
   0 0  0 72  18  arcto fourpops
   fill } def

/moon
{ .6 setgray                       % set gray level
   81 45 18 0 360 arc fill         % draw a circle
   } def                           % end of definition

/omaha
{ 1 setgray
   0 −1 moveto
   1 2 scale                       % double y-scale
   (OMAHA) stringwidth pop         % width of word
   108 exch sub 2 div              % calc. indentation
   0 rmoveto                       % indent
   (OMAHA) show } def              % & print

% ------------ Begin Program ----------------
255 465 translate

background
moon
omaha

showpage
```

This program follows the usual pattern of defining a series of procedures and then later calling them in sequence at the end of the source code.

The first three procedures are reasonably straightforward. *Fourpops* drops four objects from the stack; this is used after the **arcto** operator to remove the coordinates left on the stack. The *background* procedure uses four **arcto**'s to construct a rectangular path with rounded corners and then fills the path. *Moon* constructs a circular path and fills it with gray.

The *omaha* procedure prints that name in white capital letters against the black background. Note that the line

```
1 2 scale
```

doubles the vertical scale of the coordinate system in use. This makes our letters taller than they would be otherwise. The lines

```
(OMAHA) stringwidth pop
108 exch sub 2 div
0 rmoveto
```

calculate the indentation needed to center the string *OMAHA* on the background. The first of these lines determines the printed width of the string; the second and third lines subtract this width from the total width of the background (108 units) and move half that amount to the right.

6.4 OPERATOR SUMMARY

Control Operators

repeat   n proc $\Rightarrow$ —
Execute *proc* *n* times

Coordinate Systems Operators

rotate   angle $\Rightarrow$ —
Rotate user space *angle* degrees counterclockwise about origin

scale   x y $\Rightarrow$ —
Scale user space by *x* horizontally and *y* vertically

translate   x y $\Rightarrow$ —
Move origin of user space to *(x,y)*

Graphics State Operators

grestore   — $\Rightarrow$ —
Restore graphics state from matching *gsave*

gsave   — $\Rightarrow$ —
Save current graphics state

Path Construction Operators

arc   x y r ang_1 ang_2 $\Rightarrow$ —
Add counterclockwise arc to current path

arcn   x y r ang_1 ang_2 $\Rightarrow$ —
Add clockwise arc to current path

arcto x_1 y_1 x_2 y_2 r $\Rightarrow$ xt_1 yt_1 xt_2 yt_2
Build tangent arc

currentpoint   — $\Rightarrow$ x y
return coordinates of current point

CHAPTER 7

LOOPS AND CONDITIONALS

The POSTSCRIPT language has many operators for specifying the flow of control within a program. We used one of these, the **repeat** operator, in the previous chapter. All POSTSCRIPT control operators make use of an object type which we briefly mentioned before, the *executable array*, a more formal name for the object we have been calling a *procedure*.

Executable Arrays

An executable array, that is, a POSTSCRIPT procedure, is an array whose contents are to be executed by the POSTSCRIPT interpreter.

When the interpreter encounters a series of objects (values and names) in a program, it carries out the actions appropriate to those instructions, placing objects on the stack and looking up and executing operators and procedures.

However, if a series of objects is enclosed in braces, it is not immediately executed, but is stored in an array and placed on the stack. Thus, the line

    86 23 add

causes the interpreter to add the numbers *86* and *23* together, while the line

```
{86 23 add}
```

places the numbers and the operator **add** in an array, which is then placed on the stack. An executable array will often be preceded by a literal name and followed by a **def** operator, which associates it with the name in the current dictionary. (This is how named procedures are defined.)

An executable array may also be used as an argument for a control operator, such as **repeat**. In this case, the executable array holds the operations that are to take place when the conditions of the control operator are met.

7.1 CONDITIONAL EXECUTION

Comparisons

The POSTSCRIPT language has a full set of comparison operators. These compare the top two items on the stack, which can be of any matching type, and return an object of type *boolean*, a *true* or *false*, on the stack. The POSTSCRIPT comparison operators, and their equivalent mathematical symbols, are:

• eq =	**• ne** ≠
• gt >	**• lt** <
• ge ≥	**• le** ≤

The boolean results of the above operators can be used with the POSTSCRIPT logical operators **not**, **and**, **or**, and **xor**.

The **if** Operator

The **if** operator takes a boolean object and an executable array from the stack and carries out the operations in the array if the boolean value is *true*. Thus, we could define a procedure for a text formatter that would check to see if the end of the current line had been reached:

```
/chkforendofline
  { currentpoint pop          %get x-position
    612 gt    %greater than 612?
    {0 -12 translate  0 0 moveto} if
  } def
```

This procedure obtains the position of the current point and throws away the *y* coordinate. It then compares the remaining *x* coordinate to see if it is beyond the right edge of the current page. If so, it carries out a set of operations that moves the coordinate origin and current point to the beginning of the next line.

Let us write a program that will do very simple formatted printing of a series of strings. This program contains a procedure that takes a string off the stack, checks to see if that string will fit on the current line, moves to a new line, if necessary, and then prints the string.

```
% -------------- Variables ---------------
/LM 72 def                    %left margin
/RM 216 def                   %right margin
/ypos 720 def                 %current y-position
/lineheight 14 def            %distance between lines
                              %  of text
% ------------- Procedures ---------------
/newline                      %move to next line
  { ypos lineheight sub       %decrease ypos
    /ypos exch def            %...& save new value
    LM ypos moveto } def      %move to next line

/prtstr                       %stack: str
  { dup stringwidth pop       %calc. length of string
    currentpoint pop          %get horiz. position
    add  RM  gt               %sum > right margin?
    {newline} if              %if so, next line
    show } def                %print string
```

```
%------------- Main Program --------------
/Times-Italic findfont  13 scalefont setfont

LM ypos moveto
(If ) prtstr  (you ) prtstr (tell ) prtstr
(the ) prtstr  (truth, ) prtstr (you ) prtstr
(don't ) prtstr  (have ) prtstr  (to ) prtstr
(remember ) prtstr  (anything.  ) prtstr
 (- Mark ) prtstr  (Twain ) prtstr

   showpage
```

If you tell the truth, you don't have to remember anything. - Mark Twain

Three variables are defined here. *LM* and *RM* are the left and right margins, repectively, within which the text is to be printed. *Ypos* is the vertical position of the current line on which text is being printed. *Lineheight* is the vertical distance that will separate lines of text.

The procedure *newline* moves the current point to the beginning of the next line. It decreases *ypos* by *lineheight*, defining the result to be the new value of *ypos*:

```
ypos lineheight sub
/ypos exch def
```

It then moves the current point to the left margin at the vertical position determined by *ypos*.

```
LM  ypos  moveto
```

The second procedure defined in this program, *prtstr*, checks to see if the string on the stack will fit on the current line, moves to the next line, if appropriate, and prints the string.

The procedure first duplicates the string to be printed, and then calculates its length by using **stringwidth** and dropping the *y* value.

```
dup stringwidth pop
```

The procedure then determines the *x* position of the current point.

```
currentpoint pop
```

These two values are added and the sum is compared to the right margin to see if the word would run beyond the margin.

```
add  RM  gt
```

If so, the *newline* procedure is called. In either case, the string, still on the stack, is printed.

```
{newline} if
show
```

In the main part of the program, the current point is moved to its beginning position and then the text is printed, one word at a time.

This is a very primitive text formatter, unable to parse lines of text into words. A more sophisticated formatter is presented in the *POSTSCRIPT Language Cookbook.*

The **ifelse** Operator

The second POSTSCRIPT conditional operator requires three objects on the stack: a boolean value and two executable arrays. The first array placed on the stack will be executed if the boolean value is true; the second array will be executed if the boolean object is false. That is, the program line

```
bool {op1} {op2}  ifelse
```

will execute *op1* if *bool* is true and *op2* otherwise.

The program below uses the **ifelse** operator to produce a stack of overlapping trapezoids of alternating gray shade and decreasing height. The height is varied by changing the vertical scale for each trapezoid as determined by the variable *scalefactor.* The gray shade is alternated by counting the trapezoids as they are constructed and filling even trapezoids with gray and odds with black. The variable *counter* holds the number of the current trapezoid.

```
% ------- Variables & Procedures ---------
/scalefactor 1 def
/counter 0 def
/DecreaseScale
 { scalefactor .2 sub
   /scalefactor exch def } def

/IncreaseCounter
 { /counter counter 1 add def } def

/trappath          %construct a trapezoid
 { 0 0 moveto  90 0 rlineto
   -20 45 rlineto  -50 0 rlineto
   closepath } def

/doATrap
 { gsave
     1 scalefactor scale        %scale vert. axis
     trappath                    %construct path
     counter 2 mod               %is counter even?
     0 eq {.5} {0} ifelse        %choose grey or black
     setgray  fill
   grestore } def                %restore scale, etc.

% ------------ Begin Program ----------
250 350 translate

5
{IncreaseCounter
 doATrap
 DecreaseScale
 0 20 translate } repeat

showpage
```

The procedures *DecreaseScale* and *IncreaseCounter* do what their names imply, the former decreasing *scale* by .2, the latter increasing *counter* by 1.

The *trappath* procedure constructs a trapezoidal path with its lower left corner at the origin. Successive trapezoids are offset by translating the coordinate system.

Finally, the *doATrap* procedure scales the current coordinate system, constructs a trapezoidal path (using *trappath*), and then calculates *counter* modulo 2.

```
1 scalefactor scale
trappath
counter 2 mod
```

The modulo operation will yield a *0* if *counter* is even and a *1* if *counter* is odd.

We then use the **ifelse** operator.

```
0 eq {.5} {0} ifelse
setgray  fill
```

We test the results of the **mod** operation, place two executable arrays (holding alternative values for **setgray**) on the stack, and call the **ifelse** operator. The **ifelse** operator executes one of the executable arrays, causing either a *.5* or a *0* to be placed on the stack, depending on whether the result of the **eq** operator was *true* or *false*. *DoATrap* then calls the **setgray** operator and fills the current path.

After defining the necessary procedures, the program translates to a point below the center of the current page and implements a **repeat** loop that repeatedly increases *counter* and prints a trapezoid, and then prepares for the next trapezoid by decreasing *scale* and translating the origin.

```
5
{IncreaseCounter
 doATrap
 DecreaseScale
 0 20 translate } repeat
```

7.2 LOOPS

There are three POSTSCRIPT operators for establishing and controlling program loops. We have already used the **repeat** operator. The **for** operator controls an indexed loop similar to the *For...To...Next* structures in other languages; the **loop** and **exit** operators implement an indeterminate loop that continues until a specified condition is met.

The **for** Operator

The POSTSCRIPT **for** operator implements a counting loop. This operator takes four operands: the loop counter's starting value, increment amount, and final value, and the procedure to be repeated. The **for** operator places the current value of the counter on the stack immediately before each execution of the procedure.

For example, the following program line, embedded in the proper program, would cause the letter "k" to be printed every twelve units across the page:

```
0 12 600 {0 moveto (k) show } for
```

Each multiple of twelve from zero to 600 will be pushed onto the stack and the set of operations run.

The numeric operands of **for** need not be integers. Consider the following program:

```
/Times-Italic findfont  30 scalefont setfont

/printZip
  { 0 0 moveto  (Zip) show} def
320  400  translate

.95  –.05  0      % start  incr.  end
{setgray  printZip –1 .5 translate } for

1 setgray printZip

showpage
```

This program starts by establishing a 30-point Times Italic as the current font. The procedure *printZip* is then defined and the origin of the current coordinate system is moved to the middle of the current page.

We then begin a **for** loop. The numbers *.95*, *-.05*, and *0* are placed on the stack, followed by the executable array

```
{setgray  printZip –1 .5 translate}
```

The **for** operator repeats these operations for each value of the loop counter from .95 down to 0.

After the loop terminates, the gray value is set to white and the word *Zip* is printed one last time.

```
1 setgray printZip
```

loop and exit

Many procedures need to be repeated an indefinite number of times, either forever or until some condition is met. Other languages meet this need with such constructs as Pascal's *repeat...until*. POSTSCRIPT provides a pair of operators: **loop** and **exit**.

The **loop** operator takes a procedure as its operand and executes it repeatedly until it encounters an **exit** command within the procedure. **exit** causes a program to leave the innermost loop containing that operator. The **exit** operator will also terminate loops started by the **for**, **repeat**, and **forall** operators. (See section 8.2 for a discussion of the **forall** operator.)

Thus, the program line

```
{(Howdy ) show} loop
```

would cause the string *Howdy* to be repeatedly printed across the page and beyond. Since there is no **exit** in the repeated instructions, this line represents an infinite loop.

To see how the **loop-exit** pair work together, let's examine the following program, which draws several strings of circles across the width of the current page.

```
/pagewidth 8.5 72 mul def

/doCircle
{ xpos ypos radius 0 360 arc stroke} def

/increase-x
{ xpos radius add
  /xpos exch def } def
```

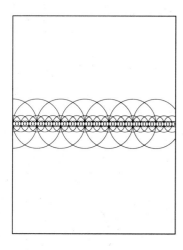

```
/lineofcircles                %stack: radius y
  { /ypos exch def            %define ypos
    /radius exch def          % ...& radius
    /xpos 0 def               % ...& xpos
    {xpos  pagewidth le       %begin loop
      {doCircle increase-x}
      {exit} ifelse
    }loop                     %end loop
  } def                       %end definition

% --------------- Begin Program -----------
10 400 lineofcircles
30 400 lineofcircles
90 400 lineofcircles

showpage
```

The variable *pagewidth* holds the width of a standard 8.5-inch page in POSTSCRIPT units. The procedure *doCircle* draws a circle on the current page; the circle's center is at *xpos,ypos* and its radius is *radius*. These variables are given values later in the program.

The *increase-x* procedure increases the value of *xpos* by the radius, in effect moving the center of the next circle over by that amount.

The last procedure defined, *lineofcircles*, requires two numbers on the stack: the circles' radius and the vertical position of their centers. These arguments are assigned to appropriate variables (*radius* and *ypos*) and *xpos* is defined as *0*.

```
/ypos exch def
/radius exch def
/xpos 0 def
```

Next, a loop repeatedly draws circles.

```
{xpos  pagewidth le
  {doCircle increase-x}{exit} ifelse
}loop
```

These lines check to see if the current horizontal position is less than or equal to the width of the paper. If so, then the procedure draws a circle onto the current page and increases *xpos*. If the horizontal position is off the right side of the page, that is, if the result of the **le** procedure is false, the **exit** procedure causes the interpreter to leave the loop.

Finally, the program does three lines of circles, all at the same vertical position.

```
10 400 lineofcircles
30 400 lineofcircles
90 400 lineofcircles
```

Recursion

A loop can be set up in a program by having a procedure call itself, a process called *recursion*. The recursive calling of a procedure can be a powerful—and somewhat tricky—tool. The program must define some conditions under which the procedure does *not* call itself.

Let us demonstrate recursion in a POSTSCRIPT program that prints a table of factorials for the numbers from one to ten. The factorial of a number is the product of all the integers from one to that number. The recursive procedure here will be *factorial*, which will define *n*-factorial to be *1* if *n* is one and $n \times (n-1 \; factorial)$ otherwise.

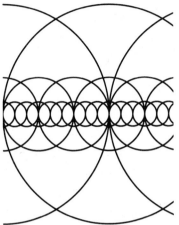

$1! = 1$
$2! = 2$
$3! = 6$
$4! = 24$
$5! = 120$
$6! = 720$
$7! = 5040$
$8! = 40320$
$9! = 362880$
$10! = 3628800$

```
% ---------- Variables & Procedures -----------
/LM 72 def
/Times-Roman findfont 15 scalefont setfont
/nstr 7 string def

/newline
  { currentpoint 16 sub          %decrement y-position
    exch pop        %drop old x...
    LM exch         % replace it with LM...
    moveto} def                  % & go there

/factorial    %stack: n --- n! (after)
  { dup 1 gt
    {dup 1 sub factorial mul} if
  } def

/prt-n        % stack: n
  { nstr cvs show } def
```

```
/prtFactorial      %stack: n
{ dup prt-n        %print n
  (! = ) show
  factorial prt-n  %print n!
  newline} def

% ----------- Program --------------
LM 600 moveto
1 1 10 {prtFactorial} for
showpage
```

The third line in this program,

```
/nstr 7 string def
```

defines a string variable using the **string** operator. This operator takes an integer from the stack and creates a new string with the specified length. The string's contents are null characters.

The *newline* procedure, as in our formatting program, moves the current point to the beginning of the next line of text. Note that this version of the procedure takes a somewhat different approach than the last, getting the current vertical position from the **currentpoint** operator, rather than keeping this value in a variable.

Factorial is the recursive procedure in this program.

```
/factorial
{ dup 1 gt
  {dup 1 sub factorial mul} if
} def
```

The procedure duplicates the number on the stack and checks to see if it is greater than *1*. If so, the number is multiplied by the result of calling *factorial* with its numeric predecessor. If the number is not greater than one, then no action is taken, and the function returns with that number (i.e., *1*) on the stack. The result is that *factorial* returns with the stack holding the factorial of the specified number.

The third procedure, *prt-n*, prints the number on top of the stack. It introduces a new operator, **cvs**.

```
/prt-n       % stack: n
{ nstr cvs show } def
```

The POSTSCRIPT **show** operator can only take a string as its argument. Anything that is to be printed must first be converted to a string. This is the function of the **cvs** operator. This operator's arguments consist of an object and a string. The object is converted into a string representation which is stored in the specified string and left on the stack. For boolean objects, **cvs** will return the strings *true* or *false*; names, operators, and numbers will return their text representations.

The string argument given to **cvs** must have enough characters to hold the string representation generated. *Prt-n* converts the number on the stack to a string whose maximum length is seven, determined by the seven-character string it puts on the stack before calling **cvs**.

PrtFactorial prints the number on the stack and its factorial, then moves to the next line.

```
/prtFactorial
{ dup prt-n
 (! = ) show
 factorial prt-n
 newline} def
```

The program then moves to the top of the current page and executes the *prtFactorial* procedure for each integer from one to ten.

```
LM 600 moveto
1 1 10 {prtFactorial} for
```

Recursive Graphics

Recursion applied to graphics can yield quite impressive and intricate results. We shall end this chapter with an example of recursive graphics. Our program will produce a *fractal*, a figure whose structure at any scale mirrors the figure's overall structure.

In this case, we shall produce a fractal arrow.

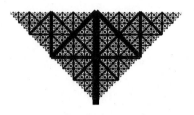

Fractal Arrow

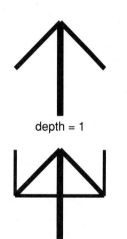

depth = 1

depth = 2

depth = 3

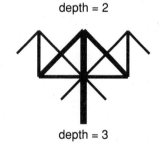

```
% ------------ Variables & Procedures -------------
/depth 0 def
/maxdepth 10 def
/down {/depth depth 1 add def} def
/up {/depth depth 1 sub def } def

/DoLine     % print a vert. line
{ 0 144 rlineto  currentpoint
  stroke translate 0 0 moveto} def

/FractArrow
{ gsave  .7 .7  scale            %reduce scale
  10 setlinewidth                %set line width
  down  DoLine                   %print line
  depth  maxdepth le             %depth<max. depth?
    { 135 rotate FractArrow
     -270 rotate FractArrow} if
  up grestore } def

% ------------ Begin Program ----------------
300 400 moveto
FractArrow
stroke
showpage
```

The two variables defined in this program control the recursion of the procedure *FractArrow*. The variable *depth* holds a number that represents the current "depth" of recursion. This variable is incremented at the beginning of every *FractArrow* call and decremented at the end.

The *maxdepth* variable holds the maximum value allowed for *depth*. *FractArrow* will stop calling itself when *depth* is equal to *maxdepth*.

The recursive procedure *FractArrow* starts by saving the graphics state and then scaling down the coordinate system.

```
gsave
.7 .7 scale
```

The line width is set to ten, *depth* is increased, and a line segment is drawn onto the page.

```
10 setlinewidth
down  DoLine
```

Note that each successive recursion will yield shorter and thinner line segments, since the scale is being decreased with each recursion.

Depth and *maxdepth* are compared, and if the former is not greater than the latter, the recursive part of the procedure is carried out.

```
depth  maxdepth le
{ 135 rotate FractArrow
 −270 rotate FractArrow} if
```

Fractal Arrow with the reduction factor changed from .7 to .6

The **if** operator's argument calls *FractArrow* twice, once after a counterclockwise rotation and again after a clockwise rotation. These calls to *FractArrow*, in turn, repeat the process. Each draws a vertical line—rotated to some other direction on the current page—and then, if *depth* is still small enough, executes *FractArrow* twice again. Each call to *FractArrow* generates two more such calls until *depth* finally reaches *maxdepth*.

Fractal Arrow with constant line width and reduction = 0.5

The *FractArrow* procedure ends by decreasing *depth* and restoring the graphics state to what it had been at the beginning of the procedure.

The image this program produces changes considerably with changes in the maximum depth, the factor by which user's space is scaled, the length of the line segment drawn by *FractArrow*, and the angles through which user's space is rotated.

7.3 OPERATOR SUMMARY

Control Operators

exit — $\Rightarrow$ —
Exit innermost **for**, **loop**, or **repeat**

for j k l proc $\Rightarrow$ —
For $i = j$ to l step k do *proc*

if bool proc $\Rightarrow$ —
If *bool* is *true*, then do *proc*

ifelse bool $proc_t$ $proc_f$ $\Rightarrow$ —
If *bool* is *true* then do $proc_t$, else do $proc_f$

loop proc $\Rightarrow$ —
Repeat *proc* forever

String and Conversion Operators

string n $\Rightarrow$ str
Create string of length n

cvs ob str $\Rightarrow$ str
Convert to string

Relational Operators

eq ob_1 ob_2 $\Rightarrow$ bool
Test for equality

ne ob_1 ob_2 $\Rightarrow$ bool
Test for inequality

gt n/str_1 n/str_2 $\Rightarrow$ bool
Test for greater than

ge n/str_1 n/str_2 $\Rightarrow$ bool
Test for greater than or equal to

lt n/str_1 n/str_2 $\Rightarrow$ bool
Test for less than

le n/str_1 n/str_2 $\Rightarrow$ bool
Test for less than or equal to

CHAPTER 8

ARRAYS

8.1 POSTSCRIPT ARRAYS

POSTSCRIPT arrays are one-dimensional collections of objects. These objects are numbered from zero, so that a ten-item array is numbered from zero to nine. POSTSCRIPT arrays are different from those in other languages in that their elements need not all be of the same type. That is, a single array may contain, for example, strings, integers, dictionaries, and other arrays.

An array in a program is denoted by any collection of POSTSCRIPT objects surrounded by square brackets. Thus, the lines

```
[16 (twelve) 8]
[(sum) 6 14 add]
```

both set up arrays. The first has three members: two numbers and a string. The second array has two items in it: the string *sum* and the number *20*. (Note that operators within an array definition are carried out as the array is being defined.)

Arrays may also be defined by the **array** operator. This operator takes a number from the stack and constructs an array of that length. The line

```
10 array
```

would leave a ten-place array on the stack. The elements of this array are initially all POSTSCRIPT **null** objects.

Marks

When an array is created with a line such as

    [1 2 3 (O'Leary)]

the square brackets play a more active role than is immediately evident. The left bracket is a POSTSCRIPT operator that leaves an object called a *mark* on the stack.

As the interpreter continues through the program line, it puts more objects on the stack until it encounters a right bracket, which is an operator that creates an array containing the stack contents back to the topmost mark. The mark is dropped from the stack and the array remains.

Composite Objects

POSTSCRIPT arrays, strings, and dictionaries are examples of *composite objects*. These objects have values that are separate from the object itself. That is, the character codes making up a string are stored in a different location in a POSTSCRIPT machine than the string object that POSTSCRIPT directly manipulates.

Note that composite objects can share values. A **dup** operation on a string duplicates the object, but not its value. The duplicate object looks to the same place in the machine's memory for its value.

8.2 ARRAY OPERATORS

Storing & Fetching Array Members: **put** and **get**

The **put** and **get** operators store and fetch array information. **put** takes three arguments from the stack: an array, an index, and an object. It puts the object into the array at the position specified by the index. That is,

```
/AnArray 10 array def
AnArray  8  (language) put]
```

would put the string *language* into the ninth position in *AnArray*.
(Remember that the positions within an array are counted from
zero.)

get takes an array and an index from the stack and returns the
object occupying the specified position within the array. The line

```
[2  5  9]  1 get
```

would return with the number *5* on the stack.

The following program defines a procedure that uses **get** to print
the contents of an array. It also introduces a new operator,
length, which returns the number of objects in an array.

```
% ------------ Variables & Procedures ----------
/LM 72 def %Left margin
/Tempstr 30 string def

/Helvetica findfont 12 scalefont setfont

/crlf          %next line
 { currentpoint 13 sub
   exch pop LM exch moveto } def

/aryshow   % stack: array
 { /ary exch def              %put array in var.
   0  1  ary length 1 sub     %loop parameters
   { ary exch get             %get array member
     Tempstr cvs              %convert to string
     show  crlf } for         %print & next line
 } def
```

```
mouse
27
aName
--nostringval--
--nostringval--
0
--nostringval--
```

```
% ------------ Begin Program -------------
LM 600 moveto

%begin array:
[(mouse)            %string
 27                 %number
 /aName             %literal
 [6  12]            %array
 {crlf}             %executable
 LM                 %variable
 /Helvetica findfont            %font dictionary
]

aryshow

showpage
```

This program defines a variable, *LM*, sets the current font to twelve-point Helvetica, and defines the *crlf* procedure that we have seen before. It then defines a procedure that prints an array's contents.

```
/aryshow   % array => ---
{ /ary exch def
  0  1  ary length 1 sub
  { ary exch get
    Tempstr cvs
    show  crlf } for
} def
```

This procedure takes an array from the stack and places it into a variable, *ary*. It then starts a **for** loop that will count from zero to one less than the number of items in *ary*. (Again, an array with *n* items will number those items from *0* to *n-1*.)

The **for** procedure uses the counter, automatically pushed onto the stack, as an index to fetch an item from *ary*.

```
ary  exch  get
```

The object obtained is converted to a string representation of up to thirty characters (determined by the initial definition of *Tempstr*) and printed on the current page.

```
Tempstr cvs
show  crlf
```

After defining *aryshow*, the program moves to the top of the page and places a seven item array on the stack.

```
LM 600 moveto

%Begin array:
[(mouse)
 27
 /aName
 [6  12]
 {crlf}
 LM
 /Helvetica findfont]
```

mouse
27
aName
--nostringval--
--nostringval--
0
--nostringval--

This array becomes the argument for the *aryshow* procedure.

Note the manner in which the different objects are printed. The string, name, number, and variable have their values printed as you would expect. The array, procedure, and font dictionary are represented by the string *--nostringval--*, because **cvs** is unable to produce a string representation for these objects.

"Automatic" Loops: **forall**

Programs often need to perform a set of operations on each member of an array. To simplify this procedure, POSTSCRIPT defines a **forall** operator that takes an array and a procedure as operands. The procedure is performed on each member of the array. Thus,

```
AnArray  {30 string cvs show}  forall
```

would print each member of *AnArray* on the current page.

We can use the **forall** operator to simplify the text formatter we wrote in the previous chapter.

```
% ------------- Variables --------------
/LM 72 def      %right margin
/RM 216 def     %left margin
/ypos 720 def   %current y-position
/lineheight 11 def  %distance between lines
                            %   of text

% ------------- Procedures --------------
/crlf                %move to next line
{ ypos lineheight sub        %decrease ypos
  /ypos exch def             % ...& save new value
  LM ypos moveto } def       %move to next line

/prtstr      %stack: str
{ dup stringwidth pop        %calc. length of string
  currentpoint pop           %get hor. position
  add  RM  gt                % sum > right margin?
  {crlf} if      %if so, carriage return
  show } def                 %print string

/format      %stack: [string array]
{ {prtstr ( ) show}  forall
} def

%------------- Main Program --------------
/Times-Italic findfont  10 scalefont setfont

LM ypos moveto

%Text array:
[(Concience)(is)(the)(inner)(voice)
 (that)(warns)(us)(somebody)(may)(be)
 (looking)( - Mencken) ]
format

showpage
```

*Concience is the inner voice that
warns us somebody may be looking
- Mencken*

Most of this program is identical to the formatter in the previous chapter. The difference is in the inclusion of the *format* procedure, which takes an array of strings from the stack and uses each member as an argument for *prtstr*.

```
/format
{ {prtstr ( ) show}  forall
} def
```

Notice that *format* prints a space after each string.

Our text can now be placed in an array of one-word strings and printed with the *format* procedure, which is exactly what the program does.

Polymorphic Operators

The **length**, **put**, **get**, and **forall** operators are actually *polymorphic* operators. These can operate on arrays, strings, or dictionaries. **length** will return the number of characters in a string, elements in an array, or key-value pairs in a dictionary. The other three operators give you access to individual characters, array elements, or key-value pairs. For more information on the use of these operators, refer to the next chapter of this Tutorial, the *POSTSCRIPT Language Reference Manual*, and the *POSTSCRIPT Language Cookbook*.

All At Once: **aload** and **astore**

Two POSTSCRIPT operators allow you to store or load the entire contents of an array at once. The **aload** operator takes an array as its argument and places the individual elements of that array, and then the array itself, on the stack. Thus, the line

[1 2 3] aload

would result in the following stack contents:

1 2 3 [1 2 3]

astore works in the opposite direction, taking several objects and an array off the stack, and placing all of the objects into the array, which is left on the stack. There must be at least as many objects on the stack as there are places within the array or an error will result. The line

(a) (b) (c) (d) 4 array astore

would leave the array

[(a) (b) (c) (d)]

on the stack.

The following program uses **aload** to print a sample of some of the standard POSTSCRIPT typefaces.

```
% --------- Variables & procedures -------
/LM 72 def

/newline
 { currentpoint 10 sub
   exch pop LM exch
   moveto } def

/PrintSample     % [string  fontname]
 { aload pop       %unload array
   findfont 8 scalefont setfont     %set font
   show  newline } def              %print string

/FontList [  %begin array:
 [(The five boxing wizards jump quickly.)
     /Helvetica]
 [(The five boxing wizards jump quickly.)
     /Times-Roman]
 [(The five boxing wizards jump quickly.)
     /Symbol]
] def       %end array

% ------------ Begin Program ----------
LM 600 moveto

FontList  {PrintSample} forall

showpage
```

The five boxing wizards jump quickly.
The five boxing wizards jump quickly.
Τηε φιϖε βοξινγ ωιζαρδσ φυμπ θυιχκλψ.

LM and *newline* are familiar to us from past programs.

The *PrintSample* procedure takes an array as its argument; this array should hold a string and the literal name of a font.

```
/PrintSample% [string  fontname]
 { aload pop
   findfont 8 scalefont setfont
   show  newline } def
```

The procedure uses an **aload** to unload the contents of the array onto the stack and a **pop** to remove the copy of the array itself left on the stack by **aload**. *PrintSample* sets the current font to the font named in the array and then prints the string on the current page.

FontList is an array made up of two-item arrays of the form needed by *PrintSample*. Each of these smaller arrays is made up of a string and the name of a font, for example

```
[(The five boxing wizards jump quickly.)
    /Helvetica]
```

Finally, the program moves the current point to the top of the page, puts the *FontList* array onto the stack and calls *PrintSample* for each item within the array.

```
FontList {PrintSample} forall
```

Note that the *Symbol* font prints Greek symbols in the place of English letters.

8.3 OPERATOR SUMMARY

Array Operators

[— $\Rightarrow$ mark
Start array construction

]   mark $ob_0...ob_i \Rightarrow$ array
End array construction

aload   ary $\Rightarrow ob_0...ob_{n-1}$ ary
Get all elements of an array

array   n $\Rightarrow$ ary
Create array of size *n*

astore $ob_0...ob_{n-1}$ ary $\Rightarrow$ ary
Put elements from stack into array

Polymorphic Operators

forall   ary/dict/str proc $\Rightarrow$ —
For each element do *proc*

get   ary/dict/str index/key $\Rightarrow$ value
Get value of *index/key* in object

length   dict/str/ary $\Rightarrow$ n
Length of object

put   ary/dict/str index/key value $\Rightarrow$ —
Put *value* into object at index/key

Stack Operators

mark   — $\Rightarrow$ mark
Push mark onto stack (same as [)

CHAPTER 9

MORE FONTS

9.1 DIFFERENT SHOWS

Printing a document usually requires more than printing the words that make up the text. The text often must be justified between page margins and the spacing between individual characters may need to be adjusted. To help with these tasks, the POSTSCRIPT language has four variations of the **show** operator that allow text to be adjusted for esthetic appeal. These operators are:

- **ashow**
  Print a string, adding a specified amount of space after each character.

- **widthshow**
  Print a string, adding space after each occurrence of a specified character (e.g., after each space).

- **awidthshow**
  Combine the above, adding space after each character and adding a separately specified offset after each occurrence of a particular character.

- **kshow**
  Execute a specified procedure between each pair of characters in the string. The current character and the character following are passed as arguments to the procedures.

For details on these operators, refer to the *POSTSCRIPT Language Reference Manual*.

We shall look more closely at the fourth operator, **kshow**. This operator takes a procedure and a string off the stack. After each character in the string is printed, that character and the one that follows it are placed on the stack, and the procedure is executed. This happens for each character within the string except the last. The final character is simply printed. Thus, the line

    {pop pop (-) show} (hyphens) kshow

would drop two items from the stack and print a hyphen between each pair of letters in the word *hyphens*.

    h-y-p-h-e-n-s

Note that in this case we popped the pair of characters left by **kshow** off the stack, since our procedure does not use them.

kshow was specifically designed to allow easy *kerning*, adjusting inter-letter spacing to achieve a more pleasing appearance. However, this operator may be used for other purposes, since the procedure handed to it as an operand may perform any operation.

For example, the program below repeatedly prints the words *Binky Inc.* until the entire current page is filled. The procedure passed to **kshow** calls the *newline* procedure whenever the current point moves past the right margin. Once the page is filled, *Binky Inc.* is printed again in the center of the page in thirty-point type.

c. Binky Inc. Binky Inc. Binky Inc. Binky Inc. Binky Inc. Binky Inc. Binky
Inc. Binky Inc. Binky Inc. Binky Inc. Binky Inc. Binky Inc. Binky Inc. Bii
ky Inc. Binky Inc. Binky Inc. Binky Inc. Binky Inc. Binky Inc. Binky Inc.
inky Inc. Binky Inc. Binky Inc. Binky Inc. Binky Inc. Binky Inc. Binky Inc
Binky Inc. Binky Inc. Binky Inc. Binky Inc. Binky Inc. Binky Inc. Binky
nc. Binky Inc. Binky Inc. Binky Inc. Binky Inc. Binky Inc. Binky Inc. Bink
y Inc. Binky Inc. Binky Inc. Binky Inc. Binky Inc. Binky Inc. Binky Inc. B
inky Inc. Binky Inc. Binky Inc. Binky Inc. Binky Inc. Binky Inc. Binky Inc
Binky Inc. Binky Inc. Binky Inc. Binky Inc. Binky Inc. Binky Inc. Binky I

Binky Inc.

```
% ------- Variables and Procedures --------
/TM 780 def      %Top Margin
/BM −12 def      %Bottom
/LM 0 def        %Left
/RM 612 def      %Right

/newline
 { currentpoint 13 sub
   exch pop LM
   exch moveto } def

/nlIfNec
 { currentpoint pop RM gt        %beyond RM?
   {newline} if } def              %yes: next line

/done?      %stack: --- bool.
 { currentpoint exch pop          %Below BM?
   BM lt } def

/fillpage      % stack: str
 { /strg exch def
   { {pop pop nlIfNec} strg kshow
     done? {exit} if
   } loop
 } def
```

```
% ------------ Begin Program -----------
/Times-Bold findfont 10 scalefont setfont
LM TM moveto
.5 setgray
(Binky Inc.  ) fillpage

/Times-Roman findfont 30 scalefont setfont

RM LM sub        %center the words
(Binky Inc.) stringwidth pop sub
2 div
400 moveto

0 setgray
(Binky Inc.) show

showpage
```

The program begins, as usual, by defining several variables and procedures. The variables define the positions of the margins within which the text is to be printed, in this case the edges of the current page.

The procedure *nlIfnec* calls *newline* if the current point is beyond the right margin. *Done?* returns a boolean *true* or *false*, depending on whether the current point is below or above the bottom margin.

The *fillpage* procedure

```
/fillpage
{ /strg exch def
  { {pop pop nlIfNec} strg kshow
    done? {exit} if
  } loop
} def
```

takes a string off the stack and places it in a variable *strg*. It then starts a loop which places a procedure and *strg* on the stack and executes the **kshow** operator. The procedure executed between characters pops the two character codes left by **kshow** off the stack (since we do not use them here) and then calls the *nlIfNec* procedure. Once the string has been printed, the *done?* procedure determines whether the current point is off the bottom of the page. If so, *fillpage* quits; otherwise, it repeats, printing *strg* again.

The main part of the program sets the current font to a ten-point Times Bold, moves to the top left of the current page, sets the gray value to *.5*, and fills the page with the words *Binky Inc*.

```
/Times-Bold findfont 10 scalefont setfont

LM TM moveto
.5 setgray
(Binky Inc.  ) fillpage
```

It then prints the thirty-point *Binky Inc*.

```
RM LM sub      %center the words
(Binky Inc.) stringwidth pop sub
2 div 0
400 moveto

0 setgray
(Binky Inc.) show
```

9.2 CHARACTER ENCODING

Computer systems handle text by assigning a numeric code to each character recognized by the system. This set of codes is referred to as an *encoding* of the character set. One widespread encoding is the familiar ASCII character code.

Each POSTSCRIPT font dictionary contains the encoding for its characters. Each character in the font is associated with an integer from 0 to 255. The *standard encoding* for the alphanumeric fonts, such as Times and Helvetica, is similar to the ASCII standard. It is important to note that a font's encoding is not fixed and may be changed to anything convenient for an application program. For details on how to change the encoding of a font, see the *POSTSCRIPT Language Cookbook*.

Many of the characters within a POSTSCRIPT font have no corresponding key on a computer keyboard and can only be referred to by their codes. Many fonts also have characters which do not have codes in the standard encoding and must be assigned a code

Code	Char	Code	Char
161	¡	225	Æ
162	¢	226	
163	£	227	ª
164	/	228	
165	¥	229	
166	f	230	
167	§	231	
168	¤	232	Ł
169	'	233	Ø
170	"	234	Œ
171	«	235	º
172	‹	236	
173	›	237	
174	fi	238	
175	fl	239	
176		240	
177	–	241	æ
178	†	242	
179	‡	243	
180	·	244	
181		245	ı
182	¶	246	
183	•	247	
184	,	248	ł
185	„	249	ø
186	"	250	œ
187	»	251	ß
188	…		
189	‰		
190			
191	¿		
192			
193	`		
194	´		
195	^		
196	˜		
197	‾		
198	˘		
199	˙		
200	¨		
201			
202	°		
203	¸		
204			
205	˝		
206			
207	ˇ		
208	—		

before they can be used (see *POSTSCRIPT Language Cookbook*). For a complete list of the characters and corresponding codes available in the standard POSTSCRIPT fonts, refer to the *POSTSCRIPT Language Reference Manual*.

Character codes may be directly used in two ways: they may be inserted into a string with a **put** operation or used directly in a string as an octal (base eight) number.

Putting Codes Into Strings

The following program uses **put** to generate a table of the characters whose standard codes are greater than 160. Note that some of the codes listed have no characters associated with them.

```
% -------- Variables & Procedures ---------
/Times-Roman findfont 10 scalefont setfont
/char 1 string def
/nstr 3 string def

/newline
 { currentpoint 11 sub
   exch pop LM
   exch moveto } def

(/prt-n      %stack: code
 {nstr cvs show} def

/prtchar      %stack: code
 { char  0
   3 –1 roll put
   char  show } def

/PrintCodeandChar              %stack: code
 { dup prt-n
   ( ) show
   prtchar newline } def

% ---------- Begin Program ----------
/LM 72 def
LM 600 moveto
161 1 208 {PrintCodeandChar} for
```

```
/LM 144 def
LM 600 moveto
225 1 251 {PrintCodeandChar} for

showpage
```

The *prt-n* procedure defined above takes a number from the stack and prints it on the current page.

Prtchar takes a numeric code from the stack and prints the corresponding character. The procedure does this by putting the number into a one-character string and then printing the string. The first line

```
char  0
```

places the string and the index for the **put** on the stack. (Note that the only position in a one-character string is zero.) The next line

```
3 −1 roll put
```

brings the numeric code to the top of the stack and puts it into *char*. Finally, the procedure prints *char*, which now contains our character code.

The procedure *PrintCodeandChar* calls *prt-n*, prints three spaces, and then calls *prtchar*, thereby printing one line of our table.

```
/PrintCodeandChar              %stack: code
{ dup prt-n
  (   ) show
  prtchar newline } def
```

The program itself sets *LM*, our left margin, to *72*, moves to the top of the page, and then calls *PrintCodeandChar* for each number between *161* and *208*. It then resets the left margin to *144* and prints table entries for the numbers from *225* to *251*. The codes from *209* through *224* are skipped because they have no characters assigned to them in the standard encoding.

Octal Character Codes

The characters printed by the preceding program are not accessible from the keyboard. They can be printed by inserting them into strings, as we did above, or by using their octal values directly in a string. A three-digit number following a backslash in a POSTSCRIPT string is interpreted as the octal code of a character to be placed in the string. That is, the string

    (785\275)

has as its fourth element the character whose character code is 275 octal. It would be printed as "785‰". A list of the octal encoding of all POSTSCRIPT standard fonts is in the *POSTSCRIPT Language Reference Manual*.

To demonstrate this method of using octal codes, the following program prints a line of Spanish text.

¡Hola, Isabel!

```
/Times-Roman findfont 12 scalefont setfont
300 400 moveto

(\241Hola, Isabel!) show
showpage
```

The code *241* in the string *(\241Hola, Isabel!)* represents an inverted exclamation point.

It should again be emphasized that the encoding used here is merely the standard encoding for POSTSCRIPT text fonts and is in no way fixed. If a different set of codes is appropriate to an application, or if a program needs to use some of a font's unassigned characters (which include a host of accented characters), the encoding is easily changed. Again, to see how to do this, refer to the *POSTSCRIPT Language Cookbook*.

9.3 FONT TRANSFORMATIONS

A POSTSCRIPT *transformation matrix* is a six-element array of numbers that defines how coordinates in user space are to be transformed into positions on the current page. The elements of the array determine the scale, orientation, and position of the x and y axes.

The graphics state maintains a *Current Transformation Matrix*, which defines how all images are positioned on the current page. The **translate**, **rotate**, and **scale** operators change elements in this matrix in order to modify the user coordinate system.

A separate transformation matrix is associated with each font, defining how the characters in the font are to be printed onto the current page. This *font matrix* can be altered directly with the **makefont** operator, which takes a font dictionary and a six-element array from the stack, transforms the dictionary's font matrix by the array, and then pushes the new font dictionary onto the stack.

In the discussion that follows, we shall only be examining transformation matrices that result in straightforward scaling of the font. Such matrices have the form

```
[m 0 0 n 0 0]
```

where *m* and *n* are the desired scales in *x* and *y*, respectively.

Thus, the lines

```
/Helvetica-Bold findfont  6 scalefont
/Helvetica-Bold findfont [6 0 0 6 0 0] makefont
```

do exactly the same thing: create a six-point Helvetica Bold font dictionary.

The **makefont** operator allows you to create condensed or expanded fonts by suitably changing the contents of the font matrix. The following program demonstrates this technique.

```
% ---- Variables & Procedures ----
/basefont  /Times-Roman findfont def
/LM 72 def

/newline
 { currentpoint 13 sub
   exch pop LM
   exch moveto } def
```

"Talking of axes,"
said the Duchess,
"Off with her head!"
 - *Lewis Carroll*

```
% ----- Begin Program ------
LM 600 moveto

%normal print:
basefont  [12 0 0 12 0 0] makefont setfont
("Talking of axes,") show newline

%expanded:
basefont  [17 0 0 12 0 0] makefont setfont
(said the Duchess,) show newline

%condensed:
basefont  [7 0 0 12 0 0] makefont setfont
("Off with her head!") show newline

basefont [12 0 6.93 12 0 0] makefont setfont
(          - Lewis Carroll) show

showpage
```

Two variables are used here: our usual *LM* and a variable *basefont*, whose value is the Times Roman font dictionary.

The program moves to the top of the page and prints four lines, each time transforming the current font with a different font matrix. The first of these,

[12 0 0 12 0 0]

creates a normal twelve-point Times Roman font. The second,

[17 0 0 12 0 0]

scales the horizontal direction more than the vertical; the height of each character is that of a twelve-point font, while the width is appropriate to a seventeen-point font. The characters are wider, the font is expanded.

The third matrix used,

[7 0 0 12 0 0]

results in a condensed font.

The last matrix in our example,

[12 0 6.93 12 0 0]

has a non-zero value as its third element. The third element in a transformation matrix affects the angle by which the font is obliqued. To oblique a font by θ degrees, set the third element in the transformation matrix to y×tanθ, where *y* is the point size of the font.

The *6.93* in our last matrix above is the product *12×tan30*, so our characters are obliqued thirty degrees.

All of these effects could have been obtained by transforming user space with **scale** or **setmatrix**. However, these operators affect the appearance of everything printed on the current page. If only the text should be expanded, compressed, or obliqued, then **makefont** is the most appropriate operator.

9.4 CHARACTER OUTLINES

Most font characters are described as outlines to be filled.

Each font dictionary contains descriptions of the shapes of its characters. Most fonts describe their characters as outlines that are filled when the character is printed. Other fonts describe characters as lines to be stroked or as bit maps.

Outlined and stroked character descriptions may be directly used with the **charpath** operator. This operator takes a string and a boolean value from the stack and adds to the current path the character outlines that describe the string. The boolean value determines what type of outline to leave. If false, the path exactly mirrors the character descriptions in the font dictionary; if true, the path differs from the character description in that any parts of the character that are normally stroked are outlined. If a font's characters are all filled, rather than stroked, then there will be no difference in the paths returned with *true* and *false*. (This is true of *Times*, *Helvetica*, and *Symbol* characters.)

(A) false charpath

For example, the program lines below would result in the paths illustrated at left, if they were embedded in the proper program. (The font used here is *Courier*, whose characters are stroked.)

    (A) false charpath
    (A) true charpath

(A) true charpath

The path constructed by **charpath** can be stroked or filled.

Let us end chapter eight with a program that generates an image similar to that reduced at left. We shall print the word *Adobe* in outlined characters at several rotations around the origin, and then print an outlined, white-filled **Adobe Systems**.

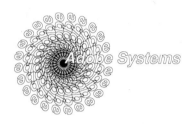

```
% -------- Procedures --------
/Helvetica-BoldOblique findfont
    30 scalefont setfont

/oshow      %stack: (string)
  { true charpath stroke } def

/circleofAdobe
 { 15 15 345
   { gsave
     rotate  0 0 moveto
     (Adobe) oshow
     grestore
   } for
 } def

% --- Begin Program ---
250 400 translate

.5 setlinewidth
circleofAdobe

0 0 moveto
(Adobe Systems) true charpath
gsave  1 setgray fill  grestore
stroke

showpage
```

This program's *oshow* procedure prints the outline of a string's characters.

```
/oshow      %stack: (string)
  { true charpath stroke } def
```

It pushes the boolean *true* over the string on the stack, calls the **charpath** operator, and then strokes the resulting path onto the current page.

CircleofAdobe sets up a **for** loop that rotates the coordinate system to every multiple of fifteen degrees and prints the outlined word *Adobe* at every rotation.

```
/circleofAdobe
 { 15 15 345
   { gsave
     rotate  0 0 moveto
     (Adobe) oshow
     grestore
   } for
 } def
```

Finally, the program translates the origin to the middle of the page, calls *circleofAdobe*, and then outlines and fills the words *Adobe Systems*.

```
0 0 moveto
(Adobe Systems) true charpath
gsave  1 setgray fill  grestore
stroke
```

Note that we put the **fill** operation inside a **gsave**-**grestore** pair so that we could both **fill** and **stroke** the character path. Our font in this program has filled characters, so the choice of *true* or *false* for this program's **charpath** operators did not matter.

9.5 OPERATOR SUMMARY

Character and Font Operators

kshow   proc str ⇒ —
Execute *proc* between showing characters in *str*

makefont   fdict matrix ⇒ fdict
Return new font dictionary with transformed font matrix

Path Construction Operators

charpath   str bool ⇒ —
Add character outlines to current path

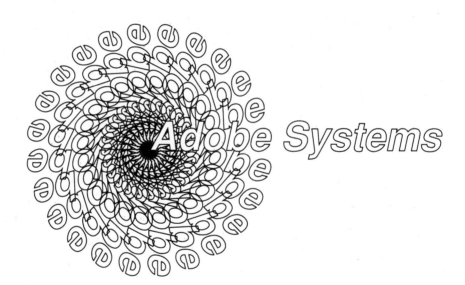

CHAPTER 10

CLIPPING AND LINE DETAILS

10.1 CLIPPING PATH

The POSTSCRIPT graphics state maintains a *clipping path*, which represents the boundaries of the region on the current page into which images can be painted. Initially, this path corresponds to the edges of the paper used by the printer. The current clipping path can be changed with the **clip** operator. The **clip** operator makes the current path the clipping path; all future painting operations will be clipped so that only those parts that lie within this path are actually transferred to the current page.

For example, the following program constructs a triangular path and makes it the clipping path. It then draws a grid of horizontal and vertical lines, only parts of which actually are painted onto the current page.

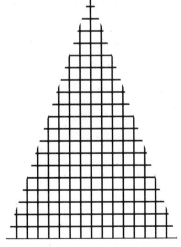

```
% ---- Procedures ----
/trianglepath
 { newpath
   0 0 moveto
   144 0 lineto
   72 200 lineto
   closepath } def
```

```
/verticals
 { newpath
   0 9 144
   { 0 moveto
     0 216 rlineto } for
   stroke } def

/horizontals
 { newpath
   0  10  200
   { 0 exch moveto
     144 0 rlineto } for
   stroke } def

% ---- Begin Program ---
230 300 translate
trianglepath  clip              %set clipping path
verticals            %Do grid
horizontals

  showpage
```

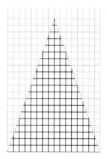

Only the part of the grid that falls
within the triangular clipping path
reaches the current page.

The procedure *trianglepath* constructs a triangular path with a base 144 units long and a height of 200. *Verticals* and *horizontals* draw a series of vertical and horizontal lines, respectively.

The program calls *trianglepath* and then the **clip** operator. The grid is then drawn with *verticals* and *horizontals*; since the imageable portion of the current page has been clipped, only that part of the grid that falls within the triangle ends up on the page (see illustration at left).

Any path can be used as a clipping boundary, including the character path left by a **charpath** operator. For example, the following program prints a series of line segments radiating from the origin clipped to the character path of the name *StarLines*.

```
% -------- Procedures --------------
/Times-BoldItalic findfont
    27 scalefont setfont

/rays
 { 0 1.5 179
   { gsave
       rotate
       0 0 moveto  108 0 lineto
       stroke
     grestore
   } for
 } def

% -------- Begin Program ---------
300 400 translate
.25 setlinewidth

newpath
0 0 moveto
(StarLines) true
charpath clip

newpath
54 –15 translate
rays

showpage
```

The *rays* procedure draws our radiating lines by repeatedly rotating the coordinate system and drawing a line along the *x* axis.

```
rotate
0 0 moveto  108 0 lineto
stroke
```

The angle of rotation is determined by a **for** loop that steps
through the angles from *0* to *179* in *1.5*-degree intervals.

The program, having defined *rays*, moves to the center of the
page, sets the line width to a quarter of a unit, and then sets up
the character outline of the string *StarLines* as a clipping path.

```
newpath
0 0 moveto
(StarLines) true
charpath clip
```

The origin is translated to below the center of the string-shaped clipping path and the *rays* procedure called.

```
newpath
54 –15 translate
rays
```

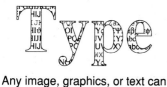

Any image, graphics, or text can be printed within a clipping path.

A clipping path does not restrict where an object may be drawn, only what parts of that object will affect the current page. An object drawn outside of the current clipping path will not cause an error, it will just not appear on the current page.

10.2 LINE-DRAWING DETAILS

The POSTSCRIPT language gives complete control over how the **stroke** operator converts a path into a painted line or curve. The **setlinewidth** operator determines the width of the stroked line. There are several operators that allow us to precisely determine other characteristics of a stroked path. Among these are:

setlinecap   Determines the appearance of line segment ends.

setlinejoin   Determines the method by which different line segments are joined.

setdash   Determines the pattern for dashed lines.

We shall examine each of these operators in turn.

setlinecap

The **setlinecap** operator takes a number from the stack and uses it as a code determining how POSTSCRIPT will end stroked line segments. For example, the program line

```
1 setlinecap
```

would cause POSTSCRIPT to paint all line segments with round ends.

Linecap = 0; Butt caps

Linecap = 1; Round caps

Linecap = 2; Projecting caps

There are three values for the line cap code:

0   Butt caps. The line segment has square ends perpendicular to the path. This is the POSTSCRIPT default line cap.

1   Round caps. The line segment ends with semicircular caps with diameters equal to the width of the line.

2   Projecting square caps. These are similar to butt caps, but extend one-half of a line width beyond the line segment's endpoint.

setlinejoin

When two connected line segments are stroked, POSTSCRIPT needs to make a decision about what type of joint to use between them. The **setlinejoin** operator tells POSTSCRIPT how to join connecting line segments. This operator is similar to **setlinecap**, in that it takes a code from the top of the stack. This code can have values from zero to two, corresponding to the following types of line joins:

Linejoin = 0; Miter joins

Linejoin = 1; Round joins

Linejoin = 2; Bevel joins

0   Mitered join. The edges of the stroke are extended until they meet. This is the default join. This join is affected by the current *miter limit* (see below).

1   Rounded join. The segments are connected by a circular join with a diameter equal to the line width.

2   Bevel join. The segments are finished with butt end caps and the notch at the larger angle between the segments is filled with a triangle.

Miter Limit

Mitered joins can present a problem. If two line segments meet at an extremely small angle, the mitered join can produce a spike that extends a considerable distance beyond the intersection of the path segments. To prevent this, the join switches from mitered to beveled when the angle between line segments becomes too acute.

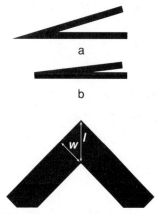

a

b

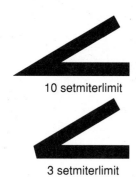

The miter limit is the maximum
ratio of l/w.

10 setmiterlimit

3 setmiterlimit

- - - - - - - - - - - -

[3 5 1 5] 0 setdash

That is, if the current line join is *0*, line segments will normally be connected with a mitered joint (see *a*, at left). However, if the angle between the two segments is too small, the connection is beveled (as in *b*).

The angle at which this changeover is made is determined by the current *miter limit*. The miter limit is the maximum ratio of the diagonal line through a join to the width of the lines producing the join (see at left). This ratio can be set by the **setmiterlimit** operator, which takes a number from the stack and makes it the new miter limit. The smaller this number is, the less tolerant POSTSCRIPT becomes of small mitered angles and the sooner it will switch to beveled joins. The default POSTSCRIPT miter limit is ten, specifying a miter limit angle of about eleven degrees.

The illustration at left shows two line segments intersecting at an angle of thirty degrees. In the upper figure, the miter limit is the default *10*; in the lower, the limit has been changed to *3*. The angle is the same, but the lower miter limit causes the second pair to be beveled, rather than mitered.

setdash

The current path is normally stroked with a solid line. Other methods of stroking a path are possible, however. The POSTSCRIPT graphics state includes a *dash array* and a *dash offset* that together describe what pattern of alternating black and white dashes should be used to stroke paths.

This pattern is set by the **setdash** operator, which takes an array and a number from the stack and makes them the current dash array and offset. The array contains a set of numbers, such as

[3 5 1 5]

which represent the lengths of alternating black and white segments should make up a stroked line. The array above would cause all paths to be stroked with a repeating sequence consisting of three units of black, five units of no ink, one unit black, five units no ink. This pattern will repeat along the entire stroked path (see illustration at left).

The second argument passed to **setdash** is the offset within the dash pattern where the stroke operator is to start when it prints a line. That is, if we were to set the dash pattern with the line

    [6 3] 3 setdash

stroked lines would begin three units into the pattern, or halfway through the first long dash.

The following program illustrates the effects of the **setdash** arguments on the appearance of stroked lines. It draws two thick vertical lines and then draws a series of horizontal lines between them, each with a different dash pattern or offset. The horizontal lines are numbered with their vertical positions above the origin.

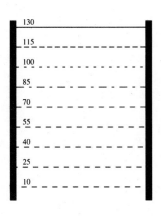

```
% ------- Variables & Procedures --------
/ypos 130 def
/Times-Roman findfont 6 scalefont setfont

/prt-n
 { (  ) cvs show } def

/borders
 { −2.5 0 moveto  0 135 rlineto
   102.5 0 moveto  0 135 rlineto
   stroke } def

/newline
 { /ypos ypos 15 sub def } def

/doLine
 { 0 ypos moveto  100 0 rlineto stroke
   5 ypos 2 add moveto ypos prt-n
   newline } def

% -------- Begin Program --------
250 350 translate

5 setlinewidth
borders
```

```
.5 setlinewidth
[ ] 0 setdash doLine              %empty array for solid line
[4 2] 0 setdash doLine
[2 4] 0 setdash doLine
[6 4 2 4] 0 setdash doLine
[4 4] 0 setdash doLine
[4 4] 1 setdash doLine
[4 4] 2 setdash doLine
[4 4] 3 setdash doLine
[4 4] 4 setdash doLine

showpage
```

Much of this program is familiar to us already. The *newline* procedure decrements the variable *ypos*, which holds the current vertical position. *Prt-n* converts a number to a string and prints it on the current page. *Borders* draws two vertical lines one hundred units apart.

The *doLine* procedure draws a line, prints the value of *ypos* above the line, and then decrements *ypos*.

```
/doLine
  { 0 ypos moveto  100 0 rlineto stroke
    5 ypos 2 add moveto ypos prt-n
    newline } def
```

The program moves the origin to the middle of the page and prints the vertical borders in 5-unit-wide lines.

```
5 setlinewidth
borders
```

The line width is reset to *.5* and nine horizontal lines are drawn, each with a different dash pattern or offset.

The first dash pattern,

```
[ ] 0 setdash doLine
```

has an empty dash array, signifying a solid line. The offset is unimportant in this case. The next three lines,

```
[4 2] 0 setdash doLine
[2 4] 0 setdash doLine
[6 4 2 4] 0 setdash doLine
```

draw lines of various dash patterns. The last five lines have the same pattern, but different offsets.

```
[4 4] 0 setdash doLine
[4 4] 1 setdash doLine
[4 4] 2 setdash doLine
[4 4] 3 setdash doLine
[4 4] 4 setdash doLine
```

For more information on the **setdash** operator, refer to the *POSTSCRIPT Language Reference Manual* and the *POSTSCRIPT Language Cookbook*.

10.3 OPERATOR SUMMARY

Graphics State Operators

clip — $\Rightarrow$ —
Set clipping boundary to current path

setdash ary n $\Rightarrow$ —
Set dash array

setlinecap 0/1/2 $\Rightarrow$ —
Set shape of stroked line ends

setlinejoin 0/1/2 $\Rightarrow$ —
Set shape of stroked line joins

setmiterlimit num $\Rightarrow$ —
Set maximum miter ratio

CHAPTER 11

IMAGES

11.1 THE **IMAGE** OPERATOR

Digital electronics typically handles photographic information by dividing the picture up into small sections and recording the brightness and grey value or color of each section. A television image is such a sampled image, as are the graphics produced by most computer systems. Each sample of the original image is reproduced onto a section of the final printed image. This small piece of black, white, gray, or color is called a *picture element*, or *pixel*.

The POSTSCRIPT language prints sampled images with the **image** operator. This operator interprets the character codes of the characters of a string as a series of bits that describe an image, beginning at the image's lower left corner.

For example, the string "AB" consists of two characters, whose default encodings are decimal 65 and 66. The image operator would interpret this string as the series of bits that are the binary representation of these numbers. That is, the binary sequence

```
01000001 01000010
```

The **image** operator interprets the bits passed to it as a description of the gray values of a stream of pixels of from one to eight bits each.

The **image** operator prints its results in a one-unit square whose lower left corner is at the origin. Thus, the image rendered by the **image** operator in the default user coordinate system will be 1/72 inch on a side. Before using **image**, one needs to translate the origin to the desired location of the image and scale to the image size required.

Using **image**

The **image** operator takes five arguments:

- **Scan length**
  Number of samples per scan line.

- **Scan lines**
  Number of scan lines in the image.

- **Bits per sample**
  The number of bits making up each sample. Permissible values are *1*, *2*, *4*, and *8*. An image with one bit per sample will print only black and white. An eight bit-per-sample image can specify values ranging from 0 (black) to 255 (white).

- **Transform matrix**
  A six-element array that determines the mapping of samples into the one-unit-square imaging region. (For a more detailed description of POSTSCRIPT transform matrices, refer to section 4.6 of the *POSTSCRIPT Language Reference Manual*.) For an image *n* samples wide made up of *m* lines, the matrix

  [n 0 0 m 0 0]

  will cause the image to exactly fill the unit square. Many graphics programs generate images whose data begins at the upper left corner of the image, rather than the lower left. In these cases, the matrix

  [n 0 0 –m 0 m]

  will allow proper rendering of the image.

- **Procedure**
  This is the procedure that produces the data strings needed by **image**. This can be any POSTSCRIPT procedure that

leaves a string on the stack. The **image** operator will take this string and interpret its characters as sample data. If the string does not describe the complete image, the **image** operator will call this procedure again, repeating until the number of samples implied by the first three arguments have been processed. The **image** operator ignores any unused data left in the string at the end of the image; it also ignores any bits left in its current character of data at the end of a scan line.

A Binary Image

The program below prints an eight by eight binary image one inch on a side.

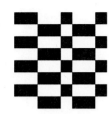

```
300 400 translate          %Move image to middle of page
72 72 scale      %Make image one inch on a side

8 8 1 [8 0 0 8 0 0] {<c936>} image

showpage
```

The first two lines of this program scale the unit square to the desired position and size. This will determine the location and size of the printed image.

The third line,

```
8 8 1 [8 0 0 8 0 0] {<c936>} image
```

prints an eight pixel by eight line image, each pixel being one bit; the transform matrix will fill the unit square (scaled to a one inch square) with the image.

The *procedure* argument in the line above introduces a new type of string. Angle brackets enclose a *hexadecimal string*. Each pair of characters in this string is interpreted as a hexadecimal number making up one character of the string. Thus, the string *<c936>* has two characters whose character codes are hexadecimal *C9* and *36*. The **image** operator will take any kind of string, but hex strings are useful in specifying bitmaps.

The procedure specified for the **image** operator in our example will place this two-character string on the stack every time it is

8 8 1 [8 0 0 8 0 0] {<c936>} image

called. This string will be interpreted as a sequence of sixteen bits:

1 1 0 0 1 0 0 1 0 0 1 1 0 1 1 0

Since each line of our image is eight one-bit samples wide, each call of the procedure will supply data for two lines. The **image** operator calls the procedure four times in making the image. The illustration at left indicates the correspondence between the data and the resulting image.

Bits per Sample

The following program takes the image from the previous example and prints it four times with different numbers of bits per sample.

```
72 500 translate

72 72 scale
8 8 1 [8 0 0 8 0 0] {<c936>} image

0 –1.25 translate
8 8 2 [8 0 0 8 0 0] {<c936>} image

0 –1.25 translate
8 8 4 [8 0 0 8 0 0] {<c936>} image

0 –1.25 translate
8 8 8 [8 0 0 8 0 0] {<c936>} image

showpage
```

The images at left, from top to bottom, represent the hex string *<c936>* interpreted as one, two, four, and eight bits per sample. The first square is identical to our previous example. The second sees the string as an eight-sample sequence:

11 00 10 01 00 11 01 10

This sequence makes up one line of samples which is repeated for each line in the image. The last two squares interpret the data as four- and two-sample sequences, respectively:

```
1100  1001  0011  0110
```

```
11001001  00110110
```

Aspect Ratio

The program below prints the bitmapped image of a helicopter in a one inch square.

```
/Helicopter
 <dd ff 00 ff 54 1f 80 03 fb f9 00 1e> def
```

```
300 400 translate
72 72 scale
```

```
16 6 1 [16 0 0 6 0 0] {Helicopter} image
```

```
showpage
```

The program is very similar to our first example, with only two differences:

1. The *procedure* argument for the **image** operator returns the complete bitmap and is only called once.

2. The bitmap is not square. It contains six lines of sixteen samples each.

The second difference leads to a problem with our program. We are mapping a sixteen by six bitmap into a 72 by 72 square. The result is that our pixels are tall and skinny and our image is distorted. For our image to be properly proportioned, the sides of the square into which the image is mapped (as set by the **scale** operator) should have a ratio equal to those of the bitmap being printed.

Thus, if the line that contains the **scale** operator in the program above is changed to

```
72 27 scale
```

(a ratio of 16 to 6), the bitmap proportions and the unit square proportions will match, and the helicopter will come out as at left.

11.2 OPERATOR SUMMARY

Graphics Output Operators

image scanlen #lines b/p [transform] {proc} $\Rightarrow$ —
Render image onto current page

Polymorphic Operators

putinterval obj_1 i obj_2 $\Rightarrow$ —
Copy obj_2 into obj_1 starting at i

COOKBOOK

INTRODUCTION

The *POSTSCRIPT Language Cookbook* is a collection of complete programming examples intended to teach you how to write programs in the POSTSCRIPT language. It is assumed that you have covered the material in the *POSTSCRIPT Language Tutorial* (the first half of this book), have access to the *POSTSCRIPT Language Reference Manual* and have some programming background. It is possible, though, for someone with very little programming experience to use the "Cookbook" effectively.

The "recipes" (programming examples) presented in the Cookbook fall into two basic categories: programs that are "ready to use" and programs that are intended as "inspiration." Many of the programs contain commonly used procedure definitions that may be inserted into larger programs without modification. For example, an application that prints geometric objects would include the procedure to draw an ellipse as presented in the program "Elliptical Arcs." Other programs are most useful for the techniques presented; they demonstrate specific applications to serve as a model for other applications or to serve as a starting point for further development.

FORMAT OF THE EXAMPLES

Each programming example begins with a reduced version of the output page produced by the program. The 8-1/2 inch by 11 inch page has been reduced to be 70% of its original size. Small tick-marks near the top edge and the left edge of the page indicate scaled inches for easier reference. There is also a scale at the bottom of the page that shows the measurement of an inch for this reduced page size.

The pages that present the actual programs have been divided into two columns. The left column is the program itself. The right column is a commentary on the program.

In the case of programs that are two pages long, the output page is intentionally repeated.

HOW TO USE THE COOKBOOK

The *POSTSCRIPT Language Cookbook* is divided into four sections: Basic Graphics, Printing Text, Applications, and Modifying and Creating Fonts. Each section begins with a brief discussion of the important points presented and is followed by a collection of program examples. The programs in the Cookbook cover a range of difficulty. The easier programs tend to be near the beginning and the more complex programs towards the end, although there is no clearly defined progression of difficulty.

Each program is independent of the others but occasionally the commentary for a program may rely on commentary from an earlier program. In such cases a reference is made to the earlier program.

The best way to use the Cookbook is to try running the programs on a POSTSCRIPT interpreter (usually resident in a printer). Then try modifying the program by changing arguments to procedures, for example, or by using different fonts. You can also try combining procedure definitions from various programs to create more sophisticated programs.

The Cookbook attempts to present a reasonable programming style and you may find that you develop your own POSTSCRIPT programming style. POSTSCRIPT is a very rich language (there are approximately 250 operators in the standard language!) and there are often many different ways of expressing the same operation. For example, the following two program fragments achieve the same result: they copy the top two elements of the operand stack.

```
2 copy
```

```
1 index 1 index
```

Many of the programs contain commonly used POSTSCRIPT programming idioms. One such idiom is the program fragment to push the coordinates of the bounding box of a character onto the operand stack:

```
newpath
0 0 moveto
(A) true charpath flattenpath pathbbox
```

This series of operators is used every time the bounding box of a character needs to be determined. (This idiom is explained in detail in the ''Setting Fractions'' and ''Printing with Small Caps'' program examples.)

You will find that efficiency was sacrificed for clarity in some of the examples (clarity was more important in this tutorial presentation). More efficient implementations are left as exercises to the reader.

Repeated Shapes

Expanded and Constant Width Lines

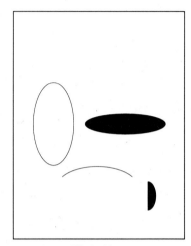

Elliptical Arcs

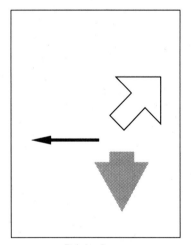

Drawing Arrows

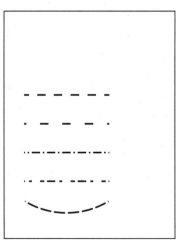

Centered Dash Patterns

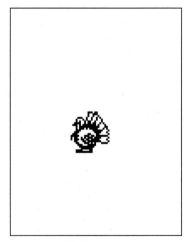

Printing Images

BASIC GRAPHICS

The programs presented in this section are generally simpler in nature than programs presented in later sections. They concentrate on the basic techniques for defining shapes, performing coordinate system transformations and printing images.

ABOUT THE PROGRAMS

The first program, ''Repeated Shapes,'' demonstrates a synthesis of many of the basic POSTSCRIPT graphic constructs: defining paths, using the **scale** and **rotate** transformations, and using the graphic output operators **fill** and **stroke**. It exemplifies how a short and simple POSTSCRIPT program can generate interesting graphic images.

The next program, ''Expanded and Constant Width Lines,'' shows how to control the scaling transformation to get differently scaled lines. The techniques presented in this program are not only restricted to lines but may be applied to any other graphic object including fonts.

''Elliptical Arcs'' introduces an important technique: using dictionaries to define local variables (see description below). In addition, it demonstrates how to build a procedure, ''ellipse,'' from the standard POSTSCRIPT operators. The behavior and argument list of the ''ellipse'' procedure are modeled after the **arc** operator. Users are free to define new procedures in POSTSCRIPT: this is what makes the language so powerful and flexible.

"Drawing Arrows" defines a general procedure that can be used to draw any kind of straight arrow. This is a useful primitive in the larger context of making illustrations.

"Centered Dash Patterns" focuses on a detail of the **setdash** operator: the offset argument. By carefully calculating the value of the offset, it's possible to center any dash pattern on any path. Included in this program is a useful general procedure, "pathlength," that computes the length of any arbitrary path in the current user space.

"Printing Images" demonstrates how to use the **image** operator, how to modify the transfer function, and how to read the data for the image from the current file. This technique of reading data from the current file can be applied to many other situations such as text processing.

DICTIONARIES AND LOCAL VARIABLES

The POSTSCRIPT language is not as highly structured as other programming languages such as Pascal or Algol. There is no explicit method for specifying the scope of variables. Instead one has to "simulate" the scoping mechanism through the careful use of dictionaries, the dictionary stack, and the dictionary operators.

First let's review some of the basic concepts underlying the dictionary mechanism. The **def** operator associates a key with a value and that key-value pair is stored in the *current dictionary*. The current dictionary is always the topmost dictionary on the dictionary stack. A new dictionary can be created (using the **dict** operator) and it can be pushed onto the dictionary stack (using the **begin** operator), thereby making it the current dictionary.

When the POSTSCRIPT interpreter encounters a name, it searches for a definition of that name in the dictionary stack beginning with the topmost (current) dictionary and working its way down the dictionary stack until it finds the first instance of that name. Due to the nature of this name search process, dictionaries become the context for the scope of names.

Local variables are simulated by creating a new dictionary,

pushing it onto the dictionary stack, performing **def** operations, and then popping that new dictionary. As long as the new dictionary remains on the dictionary stack, we will find the "local" value for the variable when a name search is done. Once the new dictionary is popped from the dictionary stack, the values for names defined within the context of this dictionary will no longer be found (although if a variable by that same name were defined in another dictionary still on the dictionary stack, that value would be returned in the name search). Methodically pushing and popping dictionaries is what gives variables their scope. The following example illustrates this mechanism:

Example:

```
/thestring (global) def      % 1
thestring =                  % 2
/exampledict 1 dict def      % 3
exampledict begin            % 4
   thestring =               % 5
   /thestring (local) def    % 6
   thestring =               % 7
end                          % 8
thestring =                  % 9
```

The output produced by this program looks like:

```
global
global
local
global
```

Description of the program: The first line defines the variable "thestring' to have the value "(global)." Line 2 prints the value of "thestring" on the standard output. Line 3 creates a dictionary called "exampledict" to be used for local storage of variables. Line 4 pushes "exampledict" onto the dictionary stack, making it the current dictionary. Line 5 prints the value of "thestring" again. Since "thestring" has not yet been defined in the current dictionary, the value in the next-to-topmost dictionary is printed. Line 6 defines "thestring" to have the value "(local)" within the context of "exampledict" and this value is the one found when "thestring" is printed in line 7. Line 8 pops "exampledict" from the dictionary stack. Line 9 prints the original value of "thestring" since the value defined in "exampledict" is no longer found.

The dictionary mechanism can be used with POSTSCRIPT procedures to simulate local variables in the following manner: create a new dictionary that is large enough to hold all the definitions made within the procedure. The first operation in the procedure should push this dictionary onto the dictionary stack and the last operation in the procedure should pop it from the dictionary stack. The following is a small example that can be used as a template:

```
/localdict 1 dict def
/sampleproc
    { localdict begin
        /localvariable 6 def
      end
    } def
```

In general it is not a good idea to create the dictionary within the procedure because each procedure call allocates new memory for the dictionary. This can use up a lot of virtual memory if the procedure is called repeatedly. The following example illustrates a procedure that creates a new dictionary each time the procedure is executed:

```
/sampleproc
    { 1 dict begin          % this allocates new VM each time
        /localvariable 6 def
      end
    } def
```

Although it uses more memory, the above method does have the advantage that each time the procedure is called, an entirely new context is created, whereas with the previous method, the old context is invoked each time the procedure is called.

There is another method for pushing a dictionary onto the dictionary stack as the first operation in a procedure without having to give the dictionary a name. This technique is advantageous for two reasons. The first reason is that it serves as a form of "information hiding" since the dictionary cannot be accessed by name; it can only be accessed within the procedure that contains it. The second reason is that it saves key (name) space in the enclosing dictionary where the procedure definition is made since the dictionary itself has no name; the savings on name space become significant when many procedures requiring local variables are defined in a program.

```
/sampleproc                      % 1
   { 0 begin                     % 2
      /localvariable 6 def       % 3
    end                          % 4
   } def                         % 5
/sampleproc load 0 1 dict put    % 6
```

Recall that procedures are actually executable arrays. The "0" in line 2 of the program merely serves as a placeholder for the reference to the local dictionary. Line 6 creates the dictionary and inserts it into the placeholder position. First the procedure is pushed onto the operand stack as an array object. Then the dictionary is created and inserted as the zeroth element of the procedure array. From now on a reference to the dictionary will exist in the zeroeth position of the procedure array. When the procedure is called, the first operation pushes the dictionary onto the dictionary stack. This technique is used in the programs "Creating an Analytic Font" and "Creating a Bitmap Font."

This program prints a rosette design by defining a section of that design and then printing that section repeatedly. This program illustrates the **for** and **arc** operators, and it shows how coordinate transformations can be nested to use the most convenient coordinate system for each part of a design.

```
/inch {72 mul} def

/wedge
  { newpath
     0 0 moveto
     1 0 translate
     15 rotate
     0 15 sin translate
     0 0 15 sin -90 90 arc
   closepath
  } def
```

Define an "ice cream cone" shape with the **arc** operator. This shape will have a 30 degree angle topped off with a semicircle. Set the path's first point at the current origin. Next, move the origin to the center of the semicircle by translating to the right 1 unit, rotating counter-clockwise by 15 degrees, and translating "up" in the rotated system by the radius of the semicircle. The **arc** operator includes a straight line to the initial point of the arc and a curved section to the end of the arc. Note that the semicircle goes from -90 degrees to 90 degrees in the rotated coordinate system.

```
gsave
  3.75 inch 7.25 inch translate
  1 inch 1 inch scale
  wedge 0.02 setlinewidth stroke
grestore
```

Remember the default coordinate system.
Move into position for a sample of the wedge.
Make the edge of the wedge 1 inch long.
Draw the wedge with a 1/50 inch thick line.
Get back to default coordinates.

```
gsave
  4.25 inch 4.25 inch translate
  1.75 inch 1.75 inch scale
  0.02 setlinewidth
  1 1 12
  { 12 div setgray
    gsave
      wedge
      gsave fill grestore
      0 setgray stroke
    grestore
    30 rotate
  } for
grestore

showpage
```

Move into position for the rosette.
Make the edges of the rosette 1 3/4 inches long.
Use a 7/200 inch thick line.
Set up the **for** operator to iterate 12 times.
Divide the loop index by 12 to set a gray value.
Enclose the "wedge" operation in a **gsave - grestore** pair, as it will transform the coordinate system.
Save the wedge path for use after the **fill.**
Draw a black border around the wedge.
Get out of the coordinate system left by wedge.
Set up for the next section.
Close the procedure body and execute the **for** operator.

1 inch
72 points

This example demonstrates different effects achieved under the scaling transformation. Normally the line width used with the **stroke** operator is scaled according to the current user coordinate system. This is demonstrated in the set of squares drawn on the left side of the page. It is possible to maintain a constant line width although the user coordinate system is being scaled arbitrarily. This is shown in the set of squares drawn on the right side of the page.

"centersquare" will draw a unit square centered on the current coordinate system origin. A square described in terms of its center, rather than in terms of one of its corners, is more convenient for this example since we will be drawing concentric squares.

```
/inch {72 mul} def
/centersquare
  { newpath
      .5 .5 moveto    -.5 .5 lineto
      -.5 -.5 lineto   .5 -.5 lineto
    closepath
  } def
```

```
gsave
  2.5 inch 6 inch translate
  1 16 div setlinewidth
  1 1 5
    { gsave
        .5 mul inch dup scale
        centersquare
        stroke
        grestore
    } for
grestore
```

Remember the original coordinate system.
Place the origin for the expanding line width squares.

Set up a "for" loop to execute five times.
Remember the current coordinate system.
Scale the current units by 1/2 inch times the loop index.
The stroked square has a line width proportional to the current scale.
Return to the translated, unscaled coordinate system.

Return to the original untranslated coordinate system.

```
gsave
  6 inch 6 inch translate
  1 setlinewidth
  /cmtx matrix currentmatrix def
  1 1 5
    { gsave
        .5 mul inch dup scale
        centersquare
        cmtx setmatrix
        stroke

        grestore
    } for
grestore
showpage
```

Place the origin for the constant line width squares.
Set the line width to be 1 point.
Store the current transformation matrix, i.e., the current coordinate system, in the variable "cmtx".
Remember the translated coordinate system.
Scale the squares as before.
Create the square path, but don't stroke it yet.
Change the coordinate space back to the unscaled one, where the line width is truly 1/72nd of an inch thick. We explicitly reset only the coordinate space rather than use a **grestore**, since **grestore** resets the current path as well as the current coordinate system.
After stroking the path, return to the translated, unscaled coordinate system.
Return to the original untranslated coordinate system.

131

1 inch
72 points

This program demonstrates how to build a procedure for drawing elliptical arcs from the basic POSTSCRIPT graphic primitives. It also demonstrates the use of dictionaries to implement local variables.

```
/ellipsedict 8 dict def
ellipsedict /mtrx matrix put
```

Local storage for the procedure "ellipse."
Allocate a matrix for the save matrix operation below; make it local to the procedure "ellipse."

```
/ellipse
  { ellipsedict begin
    /endangle exch def
    /startangle exch def
    /yrad exch def
    /xrad exch def
    /y exch def
    /x exch def
```

"ellipse" adds a counter-clockwise segment of an elliptical arc to the current path. It takes six operands: the x and y coordinates of the center of the ellipse (the center is defined as the point of intersection of the major and minor axes), the "radius" of the ellipse in the x direction, the "radius" of the ellipse in the y direction, the starting angle of the elliptical arc and the ending angle of the elliptical arc. Since the first operation in this procedure pushes "ellipsedict" onto the dictionary stack and the last pops that dictionary from the dictionary stack, all **def** operations are local in scope.

The basic strategy for defining the ellipse is to translate to the center of the ellipse, scale the user coordinate system by the x and y radius values, and then add a circular arc, centered at the origin with a 1 unit radius to the current path. We will be transforming the user coordinate system with the **translate** and **rotate** operators to add the elliptical arc segment but we don't want these transformations to affect other parts of the program. In other words, we would like to isolate the effect of the transformations. Usually the **gsave** and **grestore** operators would be ideal candidates for this task. Unfortunately **gsave** and **grestore** are inappropriate for this situation because they do not save the arc segment that has been added to the path. Instead we will isolate the effect of the transformations by saving the current transformation matrix and restoring it explicitly after adding the elliptical arc to the path.

```
    /savematrix mtrx currentmatrix def
    x y translate
    xrad yrad scale
    0 0 1 startangle endangle arc
    savematrix setmatrix
  end
} def
```

Save the current transformation.
Translate to the center of the ellipse.
Scale by the x and y radius values.
Add the arc segment to the path.
Restore the transformation.

1 inch
72 points

```
newpath
  144 400 72 144 0 360 ellipse
stroke
```

Draw a full ellipse and outline it with a **stroke.** Note that the y-axis is longer than the x-axis.

```
newpath
  400 400 144 36 0 360 ellipse
fill
```

Draw a full ellipse and **fill** it with black. Note that the y-axis is shorter than the x-axis.

```
newpath
  300 180 144 72 30 150 ellipse
stroke
```

Draw a portion of an elliptical arc and outline it with a **stroke.**

```
newpath
  480 150 30 50 270 90 ellipse
fill
```

Draw a portion of an elliptical arc and **fill** it with black. Note that although the path is not explicitly closed by the "ellipse" procedure, the **fill** operation implicitly closes the path for us.

```
showpage
```

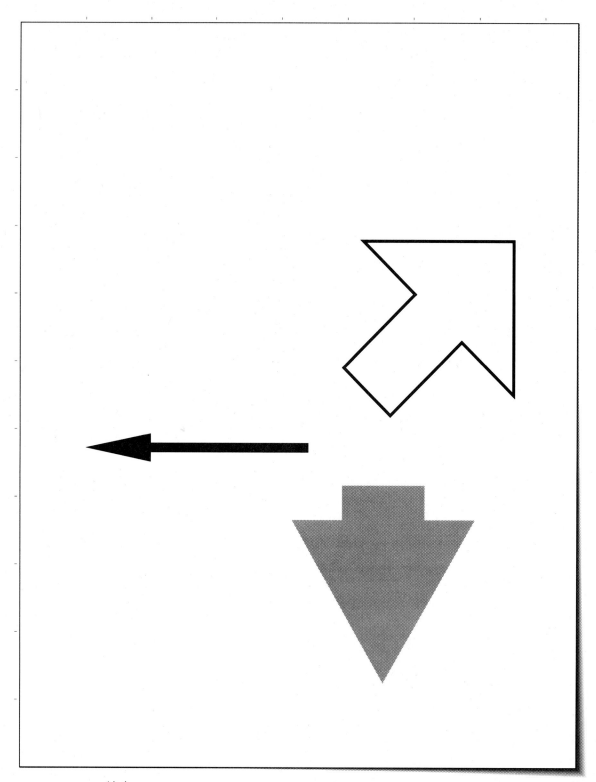

1 inch
72 points

This program demonstrates how to define a general procedure for drawing various kinds of straight arrows.

```
/arrowdict 14 dict def
arrowdict begin
  /mtrx matrix def
end
```

Local storage for the procedure "arrow."
Allocate a matrix for storing the current matrix below.
Make it local to the procedure "arrow."

```
/arrow
  { arrowdict begin
    /headlength exch def
    /halfheadthickness exch 2 div def
    /halfthickness exch 2 div def
    /tipy exch def /tipx exch def
    /taily exch def /tailx exch def


    /dx tipx tailx sub def
    /dy tipy taily sub def
    /arrowlength dx dx mul dy dy mul add
      sqrt def
    /angle dy dx atan def
    /base arrowlength headlength sub def

    /savematrix mtrx currentmatrix def
```

"arrow" adds an arrow shape to the current path. It takes seven arguments: the x and y coordinates of the tail (imagine that a line has been drawn down the center of the arrow from the tip to the tail, then x and y lie on this line), the x and y coordinates of the tip of the arrow, the thickness of the arrow in the tail portion, the thickness of the arrow at the widest part of the arrowhead and the length of the arrowhead.

Compute the differences in x and y for the tip and tail. These will be used to compute the length of the arrow and to compute the angle of direction that the arrow is facing with respect to the current user coordinate system origin.
Compute where the arrowhead joins the tail.

Save the current user coordinate system. We are using the same technique to isolate the effect of transformations as was used in the program to draw elliptical arcs.

```
    tailx taily translate
    angle rotate

    0 halfthickness neg moveto
    base halfthickness neg lineto
    base halfheadthickness neg lineto
    arrowlength 0 lineto
    base halfheadthickness lineto
    base halfthickness lineto
    0 halfthickness lineto
    closepath


    savematrix setmatrix
  end
} def
```

Translate to the starting point of the tail.
Rotate the x-axis to align with the center line of the arrow.
Add the arrow shape to the current path.

Restore the current user coordinate system.

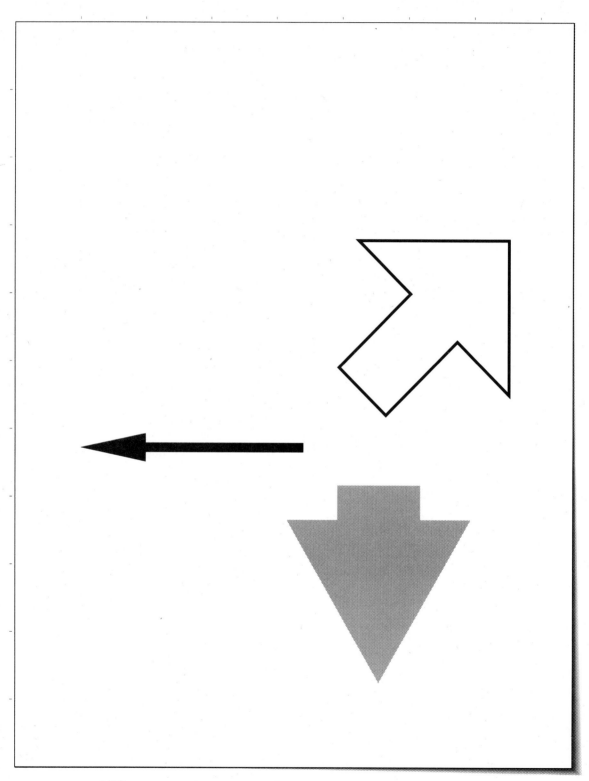

1 inch
72 points

(continued)

```
newpath
 318 340 72 340 10 30 72 arrow
fill
```

Draw a filled arrow with a thin tail and a long arrowhead.

```
newpath
 382 400 542 560 72 232 116 arrow
3 setlinewidth stroke
```

Draw an outlined arrow with a 90 degree angle at the tip. To get a 90 degree angle, the ''headthickness'' should be twice the ''headlength.''

```
newpath
 400 300 400 90 90 200 200 3 sqrt mul 2 div
  arrow .65 setgray fill
showpage
```

Draw a gray-filled arrow that has an equilateral triangle as its arrowhead. To get an equilateral triangle, the ''headlength'' should be the square root of 3 divided by 2 times the ''headthickness.''

This program demonstrates the use of the offset argument to the **setdash** operator to center any dash pattern on a continuous path. The algorithm presented will not give the expected results if the path is discontinuous or closed. Included in this example is a very useful procedure, "pathlength," that computes the length of an arbitrary path.

```
/centerdash
  { /pattern exch def
```

The procedure "centerdash" will center a dash pattern on a path such that the dashes at the end points are identical. It takes an array describing the dash pattern as its argument.

```
  /pathlen pathlength def
```

In order to center the dash pattern on the path we need to determine the length of the path. (See the definition of "pathlength" below.)

```
  /patternlength 0 def
  pattern
    { patternlength add /patternlength exch def
    } forall
```

First determine the total length of the repeating pattern by summing the elements of the dash array.

```
  pattern length 2 mod 0 ne
    { /patternlength patternlength 2 mul def } if
```

If the pattern array is an odd number of elements, double the pattern length so that we can get identical end points.

```
  /first pattern 0 get def
```

Get the length of the first element in the pattern array for use later.

```
  /last patternlength first sub def
```

Calculate the length of the remaining part of the pattern.

```
  /n pathlen last sub patternlength idiv def
  /endpart pathlen patternlength n mul sub
    last sub 2 div def
```

Now calculate the offset provided to the **setdash** operator so that the dashes at the end points are identical. Think of the path as being composed of 4 distinct parts: 2 identical end parts, 1 part which is composed of "n" repeating pattern pieces and 1 part which is the remaining piece of the pattern. We can compute the lengths of the remaining piece and the part composed of "n" repeating pattern pieces and from these determine the length of the end part.

```
  /offset first endpart sub def
```

The amount of offset is then given by the difference in length of the first part and the end part.

```
  pattern offset setdash
} def
```

Set up the dashing parameters using the offset computed above.

(continued)

```
/pathlength
  { flattenpath
    /dist 0 def




    { /yfirst exch def /xfirst exch def
      /ymoveto yfirst def /xmoveto xfirst def }
    { /ynext exch def /xnext exch def
      /dist dist ynext yfirst sub dup mul
        xnext xfirst sub dup mul add sqrt add def
      /yfirst ynext def /xfirst xnext def}
    {}


    { /ynext ymoveto def /xnext xmoveto def
      /dist dist ynext yfirst sub dup mul
        xnext xfirst sub dup mul add sqrt add def
      /yfirst ynext def /xfirst xnext def}
    pathforall
    dist
  } def
```

The procedure "pathlength" computes the length of any given path. It does so by first "flattening" the path with the **flattenpath** operator. **flattenpath** converts any **curveto** and **arc** segments in a path to a series of **lineto** segments. Then the **pathforall** operator is used to access each segment in the path, find its length and add the length to a total.

Remember the coordinates of the most recent **moveto** so that the length of the **closepath** can be computed. For each **lineto** segment, compute the distance between the current point and the previous point.

The **curveto** procedure does nothing since there shouldn't be any **curveto** segments in the path after a **flattenpath.**

The coordinates for a **closepath** segment are the coordinates of the most recent **moveto.**

Leave the length of the path on the operand stack.

```
5 setlinewidth
```

Set up the line width.

```
newpath
  72 500 moveto 378 500 lineto
[30] centerdash  stroke
```

Center a very simple dash pattern in which the unfilled dashes have the same length as the filled ones.

```
newpath
  72 400 moveto 378 400 lineto
[30 50] centerdash  stroke
```

Center a pattern which is similar to the above example except that the unfilled dashes are longer than the filled ones.

```
newpath
  72 300 moveto 378 300 lineto
[30 10 5 10] centerdash  stroke
```

Center a dot-dash pattern.

```
newpath
  72 200 moveto 378 200 lineto
[30 15 10] centerdash  stroke
```

Center an asymmetric pattern.

```
newpath
  225 390 300 240 300 arc
[40 10] centerdash  stroke
showpage
```

Center a dash pattern on an arbitrary continuous path, in this case an arc.

1 inch
72 points

This program demonstrates the use of the **image** operator. It also shows a useful technique for reading the data for the image from the current file. An important general procedure, ''concatprocs,'' is defined and used in redefining the transfer function.

```
/concatprocs
  { /proc2 exch cvlit def
    /proc1 exch cvlit def


    /newproc proc1 length proc2 length add
      array def
    newproc 0 proc1 putinterval
    newproc proc1 length proc2 putinterval
    newproc cvx
  } def

/inch { 72 mul } def
/picstr 3 string def


/imageturkey
  { 24 23 1 [24 0 0 -23 0 23]
    { currentfile picstr readhexstring pop }
    image
  } def
```

''concatprocs'' takes two procedure bodies as arguments and concatenates them into one procedure body. The resulting procedure body is left on the operand stack. ''concatprocs'' will be used in constructing a new transfer function below.
Create a new array large enough to accommodate both procedures.
Place the 1st procedure at the beginning of the new one.
Place the second procedure at the end of the new one.
Now make this array into an executable object.

String used in reading hexadecimal strings below (each row is 3 bytes long).

The procedure ''imageturkey'' reads the image (as hexadecimal strings) from this file and prints it on the page. The image of the turkey is represented as one bit per sample. It is 24 samples wide by 23 samples high and its first sample is in the upper left corner of the source image.

The image we generate is mapped to the unit square in user space. This unit square has its lower left corner at the origin and extends 1 unit in the positive x and y directions. Translate the user space origin to center the image on the page. Then scale the coordinate system to get a larger unit square.

```
gsave
  3 inch 4 inch translate
  2 inch dup scale
```

Isolate the effects of the **settransfer.**
Position the unit square on the page.
Scale it to be 2 inches square.

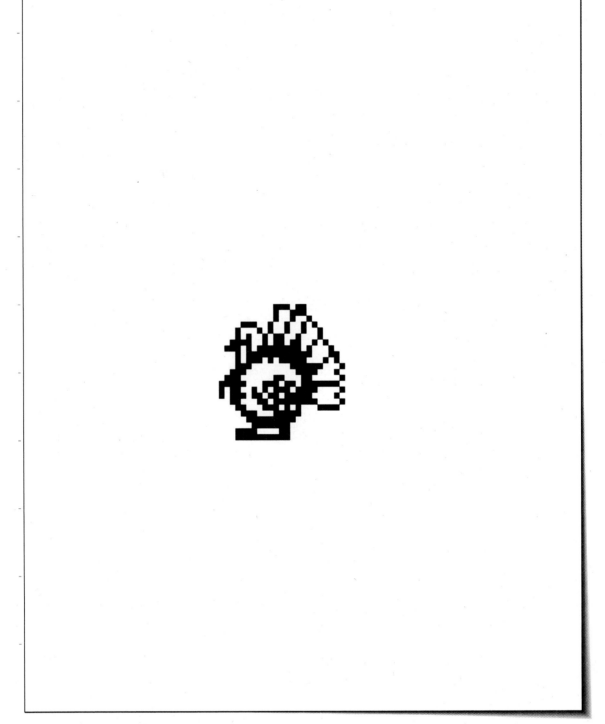

1 inch
72 points

(continued)

{1 exch sub} currenttransfer concatprocs
  settransfer

Since the source samples for our image specify a reverse image (that is, the samples that correspond to "black" are specified as 1's rather than 0's) we specify a transfer function to reverse this effect. Since some output devices have complex transfer functions we don't simply want to set the transfer function. Instead we want to concatenate our new transfer function with the existing one to achieve our results.

imageturkey
003B00 002700 002480 0E4940
114920 14B220 3CB650 75FE88
17FF8C 175F14 1C07E2 3803C4
703182 F8EDFC B2BBC2 BB6F84
31BFC2 18EA3C 0E3E00 07FC00
03F800 1E1800 1FF800

As soon as "imageturkey" is executed, the **currentfile** ... **readhexstring** sequence will begin reading bytes from this file. The safest way to synchronize reading from the program file with the POSTSCRIPT interpreter's own reading of this file is to embed the reading commands in a procedure, then place that procedure name followed by a "carriage return" followed by the bytes to be read in the file. In the hexadecimal string specified here, each series of 6 hexadecimal numbers represents a row of bits in the turkey bitmap. Each hexadecimal character represents a pattern of four 0's or 1's where 0's are black and 1's are white. Notice that this image is specified as a "reverse" image since the turkey is white and the background is black.

grestore
showpage

The **image** command reads exactly the number of bytes we supplied, and the interpreter picks up its reading here.

To read means to obtain meaning from words, and
legibility is THAT QUALITY WHICH enables words
to be read easily, quickly, and accurately.

JOHN C. TARR

Printing with Small Caps

$^{13}/_{22}$

Slowly stir in 5½ lbs. of chocolate and then blend on high.

¾

$^{7}/_{8}$

Setting Fractions

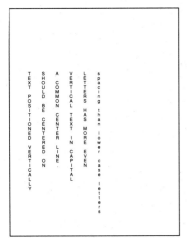

Vertical Text

Circular Text

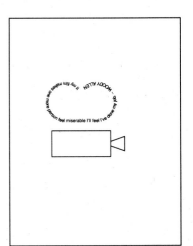

Placing Text Along an Arbitrary Path

PRINTING TEXT

The programs in this section contain procedures that are very useful in typesetting. They also provide guidelines for sophisticated typography. The fonts available through the POSTSCRIPT language give us a great deal of flexibility since they can be arbitrarily scaled and rotated. Without this flexibility, most of these programs could not be written. Most of the programs in this section are fairly short and simple since the POSTSCRIPT language has an extensive set of operators for manipulating fonts and printing text.

ABOUT THE PROGRAMS

The program ''Printing with Small Caps'' defines a general procedure called ''scshow'' for printing a string of capital letters as *small caps* in the current font. In traditional typography, small caps are capital letters that have been designed to match the x-height of a particular typeface; they are smaller in height than regular capital letters. The ''scshow'' procedure generates small caps of the proper proportions to coordinate with the current font. In order to get the proper proportions, the font must be scaled anamorphically; this is accomplished using the **makefont** operator.

''Printing with Small Caps'' also illustrates an important technique for computing the bounding box of a character. Since the proportions used for the size of the small caps are derived from a ratio of the cap height to the x-height of the font, these two quantities must be determined. By finding the bounding box of the capital X and the lowercase x, we can determine the cap height and x-height respectively.

''Setting Fractions'' defines a general procedure called ''fractionshow'' that prints a fraction in the current font given the numerator and denominator of the fraction. The numerals used to print the numerator and denominator are smaller in size than the standard numerals in a font. Once again the **makefont** operator is used to scale the current font anamorphically to get the proper proportions.

''Vertical Text'' defines a general procedure, ''vshow,'' for printing a string vertically on the page. Such a procedure is useful in labeling graphs and illustrations. The output of the program demonstrates that text printed vertically tends to look better when the text consists of capital letters only.

''Circular Text'' defines two procedures for printing text along a circular arc. The flexibility of the POSTSCRIPT fonts makes this example possible since characters can be printed at any arbitrary angle of rotation.

''Placing Text Along an Arbitrary Path'' carries the circular text idea one step further and defines a procedure to print text along a path of arbitrary shape.

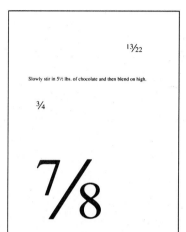

To read means to obtain meaning from words, and legibility is THAT QUALITY WHICH enables words to be read easily, quickly, and accurately.

JOHN C. TARR

Printing with Small Caps

Setting Fractions

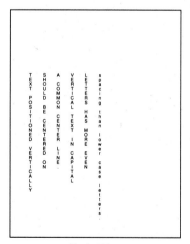

Vertical Text

Circular Text

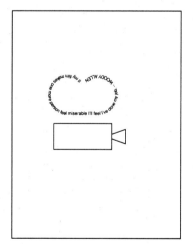

Placing Text Along an Arbitrary Path

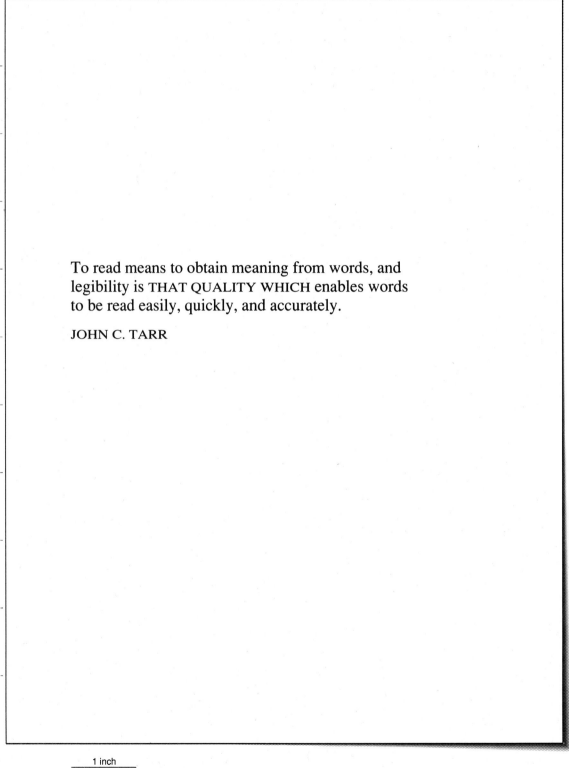

To read means to obtain meaning from words, and
legibility is THAT QUALITY WHICH enables words
to be read easily, quickly, and accurately.

JOHN C. TARR

1 inch
72 points

This program defines a general procedure for printing with small caps.

```
/scdict 3 dict def
/scshow
  { scdict begin
```

Local storage for the procedure "scshow."
"scshow" takes one argument, a string, and shows it as small caps for the current font. It makes the assumption that the characters in the string are upper case letters (i.e., it does not convert characters from lower case to upper case).

```
    gsave
```

Save the current graphics state so that changes made to the current font are localized to this procedure.

```
      currentfont [.9 0 0 findscscale 0 0] makefont
        setfont
```

Scale the current font by 90 percent in the x-direction and to the proper size in the y-direction (see the "findscale" procedure below).

```
      show
      currentpoint
    grestore
    moveto
    end
  } def
```

Show the string.
Upon exiting this procedure, we would like the current point to be just after the last small cap character shown so that "scshow" behaves like the **show** operator.
Unfortunately performing the **grestore** will return us to our position on the page before the small cap string was shown. To avoid this side-effect, push the current point onto the operand stack before performing the **grestore** operation and then move to that point before exiting the procedure.

```
scdict begin
  /findscscale
    { gsave
        newpath
          0 0 moveto
          (X) true charpath
        flattenpath
        pathbbox /capheight exch def pop pop pop
        newpath
          0 0 moveto
          (x) true charpath
        flattenpath
        pathbbox /xheight exch def pop pop pop
      grestore
```

"findscscale" determines the correct scale factor for deriving small caps to coordinate with the current font. The height of the small caps should be the x-height (i.e., the height of a lower case x) plus one third of the difference between the x-height and the cap height. The cap height and x-height are found using the following method: Create a new path and set the current point to be the origin. Then execute the **charpath** operator to add a description of the character to the current path.
The **flattenpath** operator replaces any **curveto** segments in the path with sequences of straight lines so that the **pathbbox** operator will return a bounding box that fits the path as closely as possible (otherwise the control points for the curves are included in the bounding box computation and these almost always lie off of the path outline).

```
      xheight capheight xheight sub 3 div add
        capheight div
    } def
end
```

Leave the scale factor on the operand stack.

To read means to obtain meaning from words, and legibility is THAT QUALITY WHICH enables words to be read easily, quickly, and accurately.

JOHN C. TARR

(continued)

/Times-Roman findfont 18 scalefont setfont

72 500 moveto
(To read means to obtain meaning from) show
(words, and) show

72 500 20 sub moveto
(legibility is) show
(THAT QUALITY WHICH) scshow
(enables words) show

72 500 20 2 mul sub moveto
(to be read easily, quickly, and accurately.) show

72 500 70 sub moveto
(JOHN C. TARR) scshow

showpage

The following is an example of using small caps in a paragraph of text. When setting words in capital letters, the results are most aesthetically pleasing when small caps are used.

$^{13}/_{22}$

Slowly stir in 5½ lbs. of chocolate and then blend on high.

$^{3}/_{4}$

$^{7}/_{8}$

1 inch
72 points

This program defines a general procedure for printing fractional quantities.

```
/fractiondict 5 dict def
/fractionshow
 { fractiondict begin
    /denominator exch def
    /numerator exch def
```

Local storage for the procedure ''fractionshow.'' ''fractionshow'' takes two arguments: a string for the numerator and a string for the denominator.

```
    /regularfont currentfont def
    /fractionfont currentfont [.65 0 0 .6 0 0]
      makefont def
```

Remember the current, unchanged font.
Create a new font for printing the numerator and denominator. Scaling the original font by 65 percent in the x direction and 60 percent in the y direction yields the best results.

```
    gsave
      newpath
       0 0 moveto
       (1) true charpath
      flattenpath pathbbox
      /height exch def pop pop pop
    grestore
```

The numerator should be top-aligned with the numeral height (usually the height of the numeral one). In order to position the numerator, the height of the numeral one in the current font must be computed. The method used is to create a new path and set the current point to be the origin. Then execute the **charpath** operator to add a description of the character to the current path. The **flattenpath** operator replaces any **curveto** segments in the path with sequences of straight lines so that the **pathbbox** operator will return a bounding box that fits the path as closely as possible (otherwise the control points for the curves are included in the bounding box computation and these almost always lie off of the path outline).

```
    0 .4 height mul rmoveto
```

The numerator is positioned at 40 percent of the height of the numeral one so that it aligns with the numeral height (since it has been scaled by 60 percent).

```
    fractionfont setfont numerator show
    0 .4 height mul neg rmoveto
    regularfont setfont (\244) show
```

Print the numerator string.
Move back down to the baseline.
Print the fraction bar (octal code 244) in the full-size font. The fraction bar character has been designed with negative sidebearings such that it naturally gets positioned properly with respect to the scaled down numbers.

```
    fractionfont setfont denominator show
    regularfont setfont
  end
 } def
```

Print the denominator string.
Return to the original font.

$^{13}/_{22}$

Slowly stir in 5½ lbs. of chocolate and then blend on high.

¾

$^{7}/_{8}$

1 inch
72 points

(continued)

```
/Times-Roman findfont 300 scalefont setfont
100 72 moveto
(7) (8) fractionshow
```
Print a large fraction near the bottom of the page.

```
/Times-Roman findfont 18 scalefont setfont
72 550 moveto
(Slowly stir in 5) show
(1) (2) fractionshow
( lbs. of chocolate and then blend on high.) show
```
Demonstrate a fraction intermingled with text.

```
/Times-Roman findfont 40 scalefont setfont
420 650 moveto
(13) (22) fractionshow
100 450 moveto
(3) (4) fractionshow
```
Show a smaller fraction composed of two digit numbers.

```
showpage
```

TEXT POSITIONED VERTICALLY

SHOULD BE CENTERED ON

A COMMON CENTER LINE .

VERTICAL TEXT IN CAPITAL

LETTERS HAS MORE EVEN

spacing than lower case letters .

1 inch
72 points

This program defines a general procedure for printing text vertically (with respect to the user coordinate system).

```
/vshowdict 4 dict def
```

Local storage for the procedure "vshow."

```
/vshow
  { vshowdict begin
    /thestring exch def
    /lineskip exch def
    thestring
      {
      /charcode exch def
      /thechar ( ) dup 0 charcode put def

      0 lineskip neg rmoveto
      gsave
        thechar stringwidth pop 2 div neg 0 rmoveto
        thechar show
      grestore
      } forall
    end
  } def
```

"vshow" will display text vertically, centering it on a common center line. "vshow" takes two arguments, the lineskip between letters and the string to be shown.

The **forall** operator allows us to repeat the same procedure for each character in the string.
forall pushes the character code onto the operand stack.
Convert the character code to a one-character string.

Move down by the lineskip amount.

Move left by half of the character width.
Display the character.

```
/Helvetica findfont 16 scalefont setfont
```

Set up the font we wish to use.

```
72 576 moveto
16 (TEXT POSITIONED VERTICALLY) vshow
122 576 moveto
16 (SHOULD BE CENTERED ON) vshow
172 576 moveto
16 (A COMMON CENTER LINE.) vshow
222 576 moveto
16 (VERTICAL TEXT IN CAPITAL) vshow
272 576 moveto
16 (LETTERS HAS MORE EVEN) vshow
322 576 moveto
16 (spacing than lower case letters.) vshow

showpage
```

The first vertical line of text will be centered around the line x = 72 and will begin just below the line y = 576.

Symphony No. 9 (The Choral Symphony)

Ludwig von Beethoven

The New York Philharmonic Orchestra

1 inch
72 points

This program defines two different procedures for printing text around a circular arc. ''outsidecircletext'' prints the text in a clockwise fashion with its baseline along the circumference, on the outside of the circle. ''insidecircletext'' prints the text in a counter-clockwise fashion with its baseline along the circumference, on the inside of the circle.

''outsidecircletext'' takes four arguments: the string to show, the point size of the font to use, the angle around which the text should be centered, and the radius of the circular arc. It assumes that the center of the circle is at (0,0).

```
/outsidecircletext
  { circtextdict begin
    /radius exch def
    /centerangle exch def
    /ptsize exch def
    /str exch def
    /xradius radius ptsize 4 div add def
```

A radius slightly larger than the one specified is used for computations but not for placement of characters. This has the effect of placing the characters closer together, otherwise the interletter spacing would be too loose.
Save the current graphics state.
Find out how much angle the text subtends and then rotate to the appropriate starting position for showing the string. (The positive x-axis now intersects the circle where the text should start.)

```
    gsave
      centerangle str findhalfangle add rotate
```

```
    str
      { /charcode exch def
        ( ) dup 0 charcode put outsideplacechar
      } forall
    grestore
  end
} def
```

For each character in the string, determine its position on the circular arc and **show** it.

Return to the former graphics state.

```
/insidecircletext
  { circtextdict begin
    /radius exch def    /centerangle exch def
    /ptsize exch def    /str exch def
```

''insidecircletext'' takes the same four arguments as ''outsidecircletext.''

```
    /xradius radius ptsize 3 div sub def
    gsave
      centerangle str findhalfangle sub rotate
      str
        { /charcode exch def
          ( ) dup 0 charcode put insideplacechar
        } forall
    grestore
  end
} def
```

Here we use a radius which is slightly smaller than the desired radius for computations. This forces the characters to be placed farther apart to avoid overlapping.

```
/circtextdict 16 dict def
circtextdict begin
 /findhalfangle
   { stringwidth pop 2 div
     2 xradius mul pi mul div 360 mul
   } def
```

"findhalfangle" takes one argument, a string, and finds the angle subtended by that string. It leaves the value of half of that angle on the stack. The angle is found by computing the ratio of the width of the string to the circumference of the circle and then converting that value to degrees.

```
 /outsideplacechar
   { /char exch def
     /halfangle char findhalfangle def
     gsave
       halfangle neg rotate
       radius 0 translate
       -90 rotate
       char stringwidth pop 2 div neg 0 moveto
       char show
     grestore
     halfangle 2 mul neg rotate
   } def
```

"outsideplacechar" shows a character upright on the outside of the circumference and then rotates clockwise by the amount of angle subtended by the width of the character.
Rotate clockwise by half the angle taken up by the width of the character and translate out to the circumference. Position character upright on outside of circumference. Center the character around the origin.

Rotate clockwise by the amount of angle subtended by the width of the character.

```
 /insideplacechar
   { /char exch def
     /halfangle char findhalfangle def
     gsave
       halfangle rotate
       radius 0 translate
       90 rotate
       char stringwidth pop 2 div neg 0 moveto
       char show
     grestore
     halfangle 2 mul rotate
   } def

 /pi 3.1415923 def
end
```

"insideplacechar" operates in a similar manner to "outsideplacechar" except that the direction of rotation is counter-clockwise and the characters are placed upright on the inside of the circle.

(continued)

/Times-Bold findfont 22 scalefont setfont

The remainder of this program demonstrates how to use the circular text procedures to draw a record label.

306 448 translate

translate the origin to the center of the page.

(Symphony No. 9 (The Choral Symphony))
22 90 140 outsidecircletext

Put the title of the record along the ''outside'' of the circle.

/Times-Roman findfont 15 scalefont setfont

(Ludwig von Beethoven)
15 90 118 outsidecircletext

Put the composer's name along the ''outside'' of a slightly smaller circle.

(The New York Philharmonic Orchestra)
15 270 118 insidecircletext

Put the name of the orchestra along the ''inside'' of the circle so that it reads right-side-up.

showpage

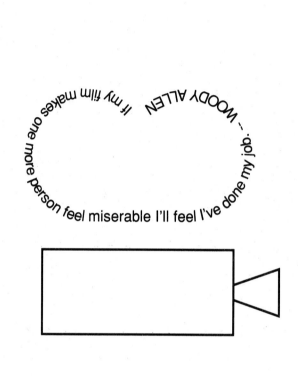

If my film makes one more person feel miserable I'll feel I've done my job.
-- WOODY ALLEN

This program defines a general procedure called "pathtext" for placing text along a path of arbitrary shape.

`/pathtextdict 26 dict def`

Local storage for the procedure "pathtext."

```
/pathtext
  { pathtextdict begin
  /offset exch def
  /str exch def
```

"pathtext" will place a string of text along any path. It takes a string and starting offset distance from the beginning of the path as its arguments. Note that "pathtext" assumes that a path has already been defined and after it places the text along the path, it clears the current path in the same manner as the **stroke** and **fill** operators; it also assumes that a font has been set. "pathtext" begins placing the characters along the current path, starting at the offset distance and continuing until either the path length is exhausted or the entire string has been printed, whichever occurs first. The results will be more effective when a small point size font is used along a path with sharp curves.

```
/pathdist 0 def
/setdist offset def
/charcount 0 def
gsave
  flattenpath
```

Initialize the distance traveled along the path.
Initialize the distance covered by setting characters.
Initialize the character count.

Reduce the path to a series of straight line segments. The characters will be placed along the line segments in the procedure "linetoproc."
The basic strategy is to process the segments of the path, keeping a running total of the distance traveled so far (pathdist). We also keep track of the distance taken up by the characters that have been set so far (setdist). When the distance traveled along the path is greater than the distance taken up by the set characters, we are ready to set the next character (if there are any left to be set). This process continues until we have exhausted the full length of the path.

```
  {movetoproc} {linetoproc}
    {curvetoproc} {closepathproc}
    pathforall
```

```
  grestore
  newpath
  end
} def
```

Clear the current path.

(continued)

```
pathtextdict begin
/movetoproc
  { /newy exch def /newx exch def
    /firstx newx def /firsty newy def
    /ovr 0 def
    newx newy transform
    /cpy exch def /cpx exch def
  } def

/linetoproc

  { /oldx newx def /oldy newy def
    /newy exch def /newx exch def
    /dx newx oldx sub def
    /dy newy oldy sub def
    /dist dx dup mul dy dup mul add sqrt def
    dist 0 ne
      { /dsx dx dist div ovr mul def
        /dsy dy dist div ovr mul def

        oldx dsx add oldy dsy add transform
        /cpy exch def /cpx exch def
        /pathdist pathdist dist add def
        { setdist pathdist le

          { charcount str length lt
              {setchar} {exit} ifelse }
          { /ovr setdist pathdist sub def
            exit }
          ifelse
        } loop
      } if
  } def

/curvetoproc
  { (ERROR: No curveto's after flattenpath!) print
  } def

/closepathproc
  { firstx firsty linetoproc
    firstx firsty movetoproc
  } def
```

"movetoproc" is executed when a **moveto** component has been encountered in the **pathforall** operation.

Remember the "first point" in the path so that when we get a **closepath** component we can properly handle the text.
Explicitly keep track of the current position in device space.

"linetoproc" is executed when a **lineto** component has been encountered in the **pathforall** operation.
Update the old point.
Get the new point.

Compute the distance between the old and new point.
Don't do anything if the line segment has zero length.
"dsx" and "dsy" are used to update the current position to be just beyond the width of the previous character.

Update the current position.
Increment the distance we have traveled along the path.
Keep setting characters along this path segment until we have exhausted its length.
As long as there are still characters left in the string, set them.
Keep track of how much we have overshot the path segment by setting the previous character. This enables us to position the origin of the following characters properly on the path.

"curvetoproc" is executed when a **curveto** component has been encountered in the **pathforall** operation. It prints an error message since there shouldn't be any **curveto's** in a path after the **flattenpath** operator has been executed.

"closepathproc" is executed when a **closepath** component has been encountered in the **pathforall** operation. It simulates the action of the operator **closepath** by executing "linetoproc" with the coordinates of the most recent **moveto** and then executing "movetoproc" to the same point.

```
/setchar
  { /char str charcount 1 getinterval def

  /charcount charcount 1 add def
  /charwidth char stringwidth pop def
  gsave
    cpx cpy itransform translate
    dy dx atan rotate
    0 0 moveto char show
    currentpoint transform
    /cpy exch def /cpx exch def
  grestore
  /setdist setdist charwidth add def
  } def
end
```

"setchar" sets the next character in the string along the path and then updates the amount of path we have exhausted.
Increment the character count.
Find the width of the character.

Translate to the current position in user space.
Rotate the x-axis to coincide with the current segment.

Update the current position before restoring to the untransformed state.
Increment the distance we have covered by setting characters.
The completes the definitions required by "pathtext."

```
/Helvetica findfont 16 scalefont setfont
```

Below is an example of using "pathtext."
Set up the font we wish to use.

```
newpath
  200 500 70 0 270 arc
  200 110 add 500 70 270 180 arc
```

Define the path that "pathtext" will use.

```
(If my film makes one more person feel\
miserable I'll feel I've done my job.\
-- WOODY ALLEN) 55 pathtext
```

Print the string along the path at an offset of 55 points.

```
newpath
  150 310 moveto 360 310 lineto
  360 400 lineto 150 400 lineto
  closepath
  360 347 moveto 410 330 lineto
  410 380 lineto 360 363 lineto
2 setlinewidth stroke
```

Draw an outline shape suggestive of a movie camera.
Draw the box part.

Draw the lens part.

EXERCISE FOR THE READER: This algorithm places characters along the path according to the origin of each character. Rewrite the algorithm so that the characters are placed according to the center of their width. This will yield better results around sharp curves and when larger point sizes are used.

```
showpage
```

In every period there have been better or worse types employed in better or worse ways. The better types employed in better ways have been used by the educated printer acquainted with standards and history, directed by taste and a sense of the fitness of things, and facing the industrial conditions and the needs of his time. Such men have made of printing an art. The poorer types and methods have been employed by printers ignorant of standards and caring alone for commercial success. To these, printing has been simply a trade. The typography of a nation has been good or bad as one or other of these classes had the supremacy. And to-day any intelligent printer can educate his taste, so to choose types for his work and so to use them, that he will help printing to be an art rather than a trade. –Daniel Berkeley Updike.

A Simple Line Breaking Algorithm

NOTE: This is not the actual output page produced by the following PostScript program. The rectangles are scaled down versions of the 8 1/2 by 11 pages generated by the program.

Making a Poster

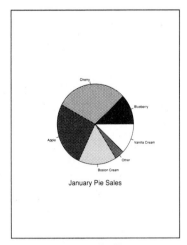

January Pie Sales

Drawing a Pie Chart

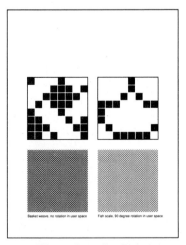

Basket weave, no rotation in user space   Fish scale, 90 degree rotation in user space

Filling an Area with a Pattern

APPLICATIONS

This section is a collection of miscellaneous programs that serve as examples of some mini-applications written entirely in the POSTSCRIPT language.

ABOUT THE PROGRAMS

The program ''A Simple Line Breaking Algorithm'' is exactly what its title might suggest: a simple algorithm for breaking text across several lines. The program takes a string and prints it in a specified column on the page making line breaks when necessary. The program makes use of the **stringwidth** operator to determine how long a word will be when printed in the current font, and it makes use of the **search** operator to find the word breaks in the string. The line breaking algorithm could be part of a larger program for document formatting.

''Making a Poster'' is useful for printing a picture that is larger than the usual 8-1/2" by 11" page size. The program defines a procedure ''printposter'' that will take the large picture and print it on several pieces of 8-1/2" by 11" paper.

The program ''Drawing a Pie Chart'' defines a set of procedures that can be used to draw any pie chart. It is a good example of integrating text and graphics under different graphical transformations.

''Filling an Area with a Pattern'' demonstrates one technique for doing pattern-fill by changing the halftone screen and then using the **fill** operator. This is a rather advanced example and it requires an understanding of the specifics of the underlying printing device, such as its resolution and orientation with respect to the user coordinate system. The program contains an important procedure, ''setuserscreen,'' that is used for setting up a halftone screen in a device independent manner. The POSTSCRIPT halftone screen machinery is very device dependent and the procedure ''setuserscreen'' serves as a device independent interface to it.

In every period there have been better or
worse types employed in better or worse
ways. The better types employed in better
ways have been used by the educated printer
acquainted with standards and history,
directed by taste and a sense of the fitness of
things, and facing the industrial conditions and
the needs of his time. Such men have made of
printing an art. The poorer types and methods
have been employed by printers ignorant of
standards and caring alone for commercial
success. To these, printing has been simply a
trade. The typography of a nation has been
good or bad as one or other of these classes
had the supremacy. And to-day any intelligent
printer can educate his taste, so to choose
types for his work and so to use them, that he
will help printing to be an art rather than a
trade. –Daniel Berkeley Updike.

A Simple Line Breaking Algorithm

NOTE: This is not the actual output page produced by the following POSTCRIPT program. The rectangles are scaled down versions of the 8 1/2" by 11" pages generated by the program.

Making a Poster

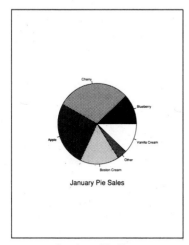

January Pie Sales

Drawing a Pie Chart

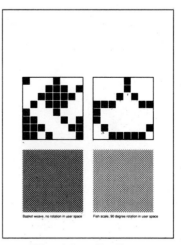

Basket weave, no rotation in user space   Fish scale, 90 degree rotation in user space

Filling an Area with a Pattern

In every period there have been better or
worse types employed in better or worse
ways. The better types employed in better
ways have been used by the educated printer
acquainted with standards and history,
directed by taste and a sense of the fitness of
things, and facing the industrial conditions and
the needs of his time. Such men have made of
printing an art. The poorer types and methods
have been employed by printers ignorant of
standards and caring alone for commercial
success. To these, printing has been simply a
trade. The typography of a nation has been
good or bad as one or other of these classes
had the supremacy. And to-day any intelligent
printer can educate his taste, so to choose
types for his work and so to use them, that he
will help printing to be an art rather than a
trade. –Daniel Berkeley Updike.

1 inch

72 points

This program demonstrates a simple line breaking algorithm.

```
/wordbreak ( ) def
/BreakIntoLines
  { /proc exch def
   /linewidth exch def
   /textstring exch def
```

Constant used for word breaks (ASCII space). ''BreakIntoLines'' takes a string of text and breaks it up into a series of lines, each no longer than the maximum line width. The algorithm breaks lines at word breaks (spaces) only. ''BreakIntoLines'' takes three arguments: the string of text, the maximum line width and a procedure to be executed each time the end of a line has been found. The procedure is expected to take one argument: a string containing the current line.

```
   /breakwidth wordbreak stringwidth pop def
   /curwidth 0 def
   /lastwordbreak 0 def

   /startchar 0 def

   /restoftext textstring def
```

Get the width of a word break in the current font. ''curwidth'' is the typeset width of the current line. ''lastwordbreak'' is the index of the most recent word break encountered in the string of text. ''startchar'' is the index of the first character on the current line. ''restoftext'' is a temporary variable that holds the remaining results of the **search** operator (see the loop below).

```
   { restoftext wordbreak search
     {/nextword exch def pop
      /restoftext exch def
      /wordwidth nextword stringwidth pop def

      curwidth wordwidth add linewidth gt
       { textstring startchar
           lastwordbreak startchar sub
           getinterval proc
         /startchar lastwordbreak def
         /curwidth wordwidth breakwidth add def }
       { /curwidth curwidth wordwidth add
           breakwidth add def
       } ifelse
      /lastwordbreak lastwordbreak
         nextword length add 1 add def
      }
     { pop exit }
     ifelse
   } loop
   /lastchar textstring length def
   textstring startchar lastchar startchar sub
     getinterval proc
} def
```

The basic strategy for breaking lines is to search the string of text (contained in ''restoftext'') for the next word break. The pre-string returned by the **search** operator is the word preceding the word break. The post-string returned gets assigned to ''restoftext.'' If the width of the word returned by the **search** operator would force the current line to exceed the maximum line width then the substring spanning the current line (from the first character on the line to the most recent word break) is passed as an argument to the user's procedure. Otherwise the width of the current line is incremented by the width of the word.

The ''lastwordbreak'' variable is updated to index into the text string at the position of the most recent word break. The last word in the text has been found when the **search** operator fails to match the word break pattern; this terminates the loop.

Don't forget to process the last line.

In every period there have been better or
worse types employed in better or worse
ways. The better types employed in better
ways have been used by the educated printer
acquainted with standards and history,
directed by taste and a sense of the fitness of
things, and facing the industrial conditions and
the needs of his time. Such men have made of
printing an art. The poorer types and methods
have been employed by printers ignorant of
standards and caring alone for commercial
success. To these, printing has been simply a
trade. The typography of a nation has been
good or bad as one or other of these classes
had the supremacy. And to-day any intelligent
printer can educate his taste, so to choose
types for his work and so to use them, that he
will help printing to be an art rather than a
trade. –Daniel Berkeley Updike.

1 inch
72 points

(continued)

/Times-Roman findfont 16 scalefont setfont

/yline 650 def

```
(In every period there have been better or worse\
types employed in better or worse ways. The\
better types employed in better ways have been\
used by the educated printer acquainted with\
standards and history, directed by taste and\
a sense of the fitness of things, and facing the\
industrial conditions and the needs of his time.\
Such men have made of printing an art. The\
poorer types and methods have been employed\
by printers ignorant of standards and caring\
alone for commercial success. To these, printing\
has been simply a trade. The typography of a\
nation has been good or bad as one or other of\
these classes had the supremacy. And to-day\
any intelligent printer can educate his taste, so\
to choose types for his work and so to use them,\
that he will help printing to be an art rather\
than a trade.  \261Daniel Berkeley Updike.)
   300
 { 72 yline moveto show
   /yline yline 18 sub def}
```

BreakIntoLines

showpage

Below is an example of the how the "BreakIntoLines" procedure might be used.
"yline" is a variable used in the procedure provided to "BreakIntoLines" below.

Use a line width of 300 points.
The procedure provided to "BreakIntoLines" takes a string as its argument. It uses a global variable "yline" to keep track of vertical positioning on the page. It moves to a specified position on the page, shows the string in the current font and then updates the vertical position.
EXERCISE FOR THE READER: If the user specifies a short enough line width, it is possible for the typeset width of a single word to exceed the maximum line width. Modify this algorithm to handle this event gracefully.

NOTE: This is not the actual output page produced by the following POSTSCRIPT program. The rectangles are scaled down versions of the 8 1/2" by 11" pages generated by the program.

This program demonstrates how to print a picture larger than a sheet of paper (8.5" by 11") on several sheets of paper that can be pasted together later.

```
/printposter
  { /rows exch def
   /columns exch def
   /bigpictureproc exch def
```

"printposter" takes a large picture (larger than 8.5" by 11") and prints it on several pages according to the number of rows and columns specified. Imagine superimposing a grid composed of the specified number of rows and columns on the large image. Then each rectangle in the grid represents an 8.5" by 11" page to be printed. "printposter" takes three arguments: a procedure representing the large picture, the number of columns and the number of rows.

```
   newpath
    leftmargin botmargin moveto
    0 pageheight rlineto
    pagewidth 0 rlineto
    0 pageheight neg rlineto
   closepath clip
```

Set up a clipping region for the page we will print on. Since most printers cannot print to the very edge of the paper, we will explicitly set up the clipping boundary so that it lies within the printing boundaries of the printer and we will compensate for this when we print the large image so that all parts of the image are actually printed.

```
   leftmargin botmargin translate
```

Readjust the origin on the page so that it coincides with the origin of the clipping boundary.

```
   0 1 rows 1 sub
    { /rowcount exch def
     0 1 columns 1 sub
      { /colcount exch def
       gsave
        pagewidth colcount mul neg
         pageheight rowcount mul neg
         translate
```

For each row of pages...

For each page within that row...

Translate the large picture so that the desired section will be imaged on the printed page. We must translate the large picture in the negative direction so that the lower left corner of the section to be printed always coincides with the origin.

```
       bigpictureproc
       gsave showpage grestore
```

Execute the large picture, clipping to this page. Since the **showpage** operator has the side effect of executing the **initgraphics** operator (which would reset the clipping region), we bracket it by the **gsave** and **grestore** operators.

```
       grestore
      } for
    } for
  } def
```

NOTE: This is not the actual output page produced by the following POSTSCRIPT program. The rectangles are scaled down versions of the 8 1/2" by 11" pages generated by the program.

(continued)

```
/inch {72 mul} def

/leftmargin .5 inch def
/botmargin .25 inch def
/pagewidth 7.5 inch def
/pageheight 10 inch def

/salesign
  { gsave



    /Times-Roman findfont 500 scalefont setfont
    2.5 inch 11 inch moveto
    (SALE) show
    /Times-Roman findfont 350 scalefont setfont
    1.45 inch 4 inch moveto
    .5 setgray (50%) show
    0 setgray ( OFF) show
    newpath
      .5 inch 18 inch moveto
      22 inch 18 inch lineto
      22 inch 2 inch lineto
      .5 inch 2 inch lineto
    closepath
    gsave
      .75 inch setlinewidth stroke
    grestore
    10 setlinewidth 1 setgray stroke

  grestore
  } def

{salesign} 3 2 printposter
```

These are the dimensions of the clipping boundary.

This procedure draws a large sign with a border. The sign is 22.5 inches wide and 19.5 inches high which fits comfortably on 6 8.5 inch by 11 inch pages (the final result will be 2 rows of pages high and 3 columns of pages wide).

Specify the path for the border.

First paint the border with a thick black stroke.

Then paint a thin white stroke down the center of the border.

Print the large picture on a total of 6 pages. The image is three columns of pages wide and 2 rows of pages high.

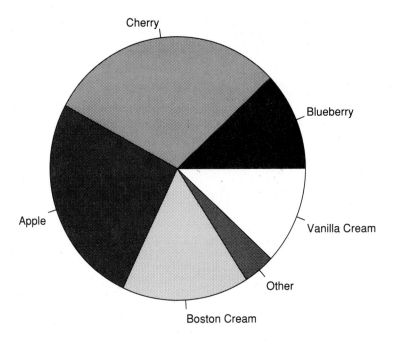

Cherry

Blueberry

Apple

Vanilla Cream

Other

Boston Cream

January Pie Sales

1 inch
72 points

This program demonstrates a small application: drawing a pie chart.

```
/PieDict 24 dict def
PieDict begin
 /DrawSlice
   { /grayshade exch def
    /endangle exch def
    /startangle exch def
    /thelabel exch def


    newpath  0 0 moveto
      0 0 radius startangle endangle arc
    closepath
    1.415 setmiterlimit


    gsave
      grayshade setgray
      fill
    grestore
    stroke
    gsave
      startangle endangle add 2 div rotate


      radius 0 translate
      newpath
        0 0 moveto labelps .8 mul 0 lineto stroke
      labelps 0 translate
      0 0 transform
    grestore
    itransform
    /y exch def /x exch def
    x y moveto












    x 0 lt
      { thelabel stringwidth pop neg 0 rmoveto }
      if
    y 0 lt { 0 labelps neg rmoveto } if
    thelabel show
  } def
```

Local storage for "DrawPieChart" and its related procedures.
"DrawSlice" draws an outlined and filled-in pie slice. It takes four operands: the label for this particular pie slice, the starting angle for the slice, the ending angle for the slice and the shade of gray the slice should be.

Create a path in the shape of a pie slice.

This prevents a spike from occurring on the interior angles when we outline the pie slices. The value 1.415 cuts off miters at angles below 90 degrees.
Fill the pie slice path with the appropriate gray color. By using **gsave** and **grestore** we don't lose the current path. Since color is painted onto the page, we fill the pie slice first and then outline it with a stroke.

The following draws the tick-mark and places the label: Find the center of the pie slice and rotate so that the x-axis coincides with this center.
Translate the origin out to the circumference.
Draw the tick-mark; make it 80 percent of the label point size in length.
Move the origin out a little beyond the circumference. Place the label at the current origin. If we simply draw the text on the page now, it would come out rotated. Since this is not desired, we avoid it by returning to the previous unrotated coordinate system. Before returning, we remember the position of the current origin on the printed page. We accomplish this by using the **transform** and **itransform** operators. First perform a **transform** on the origin to push the coordinates of the origin in device space onto the operand stack. Then perform a **grestore** to return to the previous unrotated coordinate system. Then perform an **itransform** on the two device coordinates left on the stack to determine where they are in the current coordinate system.

Make some adjustments so that the label text won't collide with the pie slice.

(continued)

```
/findgray
  { /i exch def /n exch def
    i 2 mod 0 eq
      { i 2 div n 2 div round add n div }
      { i 1 add 2 div n div }
      ifelse
  } def
end
```

"findgray" calculates the gray value for a slice. It takes two arguments: the total number of slices and the current slice number (Given that there are n pie slices, the slices are "numbered" from 1 to n). The gray values for the pie slices range evenly from white to black (i.e., the values provided to **setgray** range from (n/n, n-1/n, ..., 1/n)). Since we don't want similar values of gray next to each other, findgray "shuffles" the possible combinations of gray like a deck of cards.

```
/DrawPieChart
  { PieDict begin
    /radius exch def
    /ycenter exch def /xcenter exch def
    /PieArray exch def
    /labelps exch def /titleps exch def
    /title exch def

    gsave
      xcenter ycenter translate

      /Helvetica findfont titleps scalefont setfont
      title stringwidth pop 2 div neg radius neg
        titleps 3 mul sub moveto
      title show
      /Helvetica findfont labelps scalefont setfont
      /numslices PieArray length def
      /slicecnt 0 def
      /curangle 0 def

      PieArray

      { /slicearray exch def
        slicearray aload pop
        /percent exch def
        /label exch def
        /perangle percent 360 mul def
        /slicecnt slicecnt 1 add def
        label curangle curangle perangle add
          numslices slicecnt findgray DrawSlice
        /curangle curangle perangle add def
      } forall
    grestore
  end
} def
```

"DrawPieChart" takes seven arguments: the title of the pie chart, the point size for the title, the point size for the labels for each slice, a special array (described below where "DrawPieChart" is called), the (x,y) center of the pie chart, and the radius of the pie chart.

Translate the coordinate system origin to the center of the pie chart.
Print the title of the pie chart in Helvetica.
Center the title below the pie chart. Position it below the bottom of the pie chart by 3 times the title point size.

Print the individual pie slice labels in Helvetica.

A "loop" variable that keeps track of the angle of arc to begin each pie slice at.
Repeat the following for each element in the "PieArray."

Push the label and percentage onto the stack.

Convert the percentage into degrees of angle.

Update the current starting angle.

(continued)

```
(January Pie Sales) 24 12
  [ [(Blueberry) .12 ]
   [(Cherry) .30 ]
   [(Apple) .26 ]
   [(Boston Cream) .16 ]
   [(Other) .04 ]
   [(Vanilla Cream) .12 ]
  ] 306 396 140 DrawPieChart
showpage
```

The pie array is an array of arrays. Each array in the pie array contains the label for a pie slice followed by a real number indicating the percentage of the total pie represented by this particular slice.

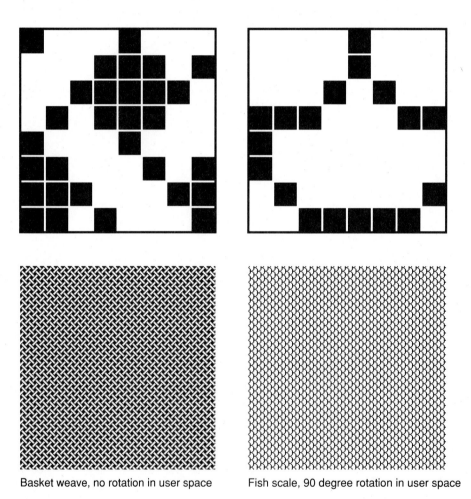

Basket weave, no rotation in user space   Fish scale, 90 degree rotation in user space

1 inch
72 points

This program demonstrates how to fill an area with a bitmap pattern using the POSTSCRIPT halftone screen machinery. The **setscreen** operator is intended for halftones and a reasonable default screen is provided by each POSTSCRIPT implementation. It can also be used for repeating patterns but the device dependent nature of the **setscreen** operator can produce different results on different printers. As a solution to this problem the procedure, ''setuserscreen,'' is defined to provide a device independent interface to the device dependent **setscreen** operator.

IMPLEMENTATION NOTE: Creating low frequency screens (below 60 lines per inch in device space) may require a great deal of memory. On printing devices with limited memory, a **limitcheck** error occurs when storage is exceeded. To avoid this error, it is best to minimize memory use by specifying a repeating pattern that is a multiple of 16 bits wide (in the device x-direction) and a screen angle of zero.

```
/setuserscreendict 22 dict def
setuserscreendict begin
 /tempctm matrix def
 /temprot matrix def
 /tempscale matrix def
```

Local storage for the procedure ''setuserscreen.'' Temporary matrices used in computations in ''setuserscreen.''

```
 /concatprocs
   { /proc2 exch cvlit def
     /proc1 exch cvlit def
     /newproc proc1 length proc2 length add
       array def
     newproc 0 proc1 putinterval
     newproc proc1 length proc2 putinterval
     newproc cvx
   } def
```

''concatprocs'' takes two procedure bodies as arguments and concatenates them into one procedure body. The resulting procedure body is left on the operand stack. ''concatprocs'' will be used in constructing a new spot function below. This procedure is identical to the one defined in the program ''Printing Images.''

```
 /resmatrix matrix def
 /findresolution
   { 72 0 resmatrix defaultmatrix dtransform
     /yres exch def /xres exch def
     xres dup mul yres dup mul add sqrt
   } def
end
```

Temporary matrix used in ''findresolution'' below. ''findresolution'' returns the resolution (in pixels per inch) of the device being printed on. Since there are 72 units per inch in the default user space, find out how many pixels those 72 units require in device space by transforming a 72 unit long vector into device space and then taking the length of the result. Leave this length on the operand stack.

```
/setuserscreen
  { setuserscreendict begin
    /spotfunction exch def
    /screenangle exch def
    /cellsize exch def


    /m tempctm currentmatrix def
    /rm screenangle temprot rotate def
    /sm cellsize dup tempscale scale def

    sm rm m m concatmatrix m concatmatrix pop

    1 0 m dtransform /y1 exch def /x1 exch def


    /veclength x1 dup mul y1 dup mul add sqrt def
    /frequency findresolution veclength div def


    /newscreenangle y1 x1 atan def


    m 2 get m 1 get mul m 0 get m 3 get mul sub
      0 gt







    { { neg } /spotfunction load concatprocs
        /spotfunction exch def
    } if








    frequency newscreenangle /spotfunction load
      setscreen
  end
} def


/setpatterndict 18 dict def
setpatterndict begin
  /bitison
    { /ybit exch def /xbit exch def
```

"setuserscreen" takes 3 arguments: the cell size of the halftone screen in the current user space units, the angle of the screen relative to the current user space and a procedure describing the spot function. "setuserscreen" converts the cell size and the screen angle from user space into device space values for the built-in operator **setscreen.**

Get the current transformation matrix.
Create a rotation matrix using the screen angle.
Create a scale matrix using the cell size.

Create a new transformation matrix by concatenating sm*rm*m and store it in "m."
Transform a 1 unit vector in the x-direction through the new transformation matrix to get the corresponding vector in device space.
Find the length of this device space vector.
The frequency is the resolution of the device divided by the length of the vector.
Determine the new screen angle based on the angle of the transformed unit vector in device space.
Merely determining the screen angle is not enough in some cases since the user coordinate system might be a reflected image of the device coordinate system. We can check for reflected images by testing the transformation matrix. Given a matrix [a b c d tx ty], if (c*b - a*d) > 0 then it's a reflected transformation.
Compensate for the reflection by flipping the y coordinate that is passed to the spot function procedure. We accomplish this by concatenating a procedure to flip the y coordinate with the original spot function procedure to create a new spot function procedure. It is very important that the flip procedure precedes the spot function procedure.
Now set up the halftone screen using the **setscreen** operator.

Local storage for the procedure "setpattern." The "bitison" procedure is used by "setpattern."
"bitison" returns **true** if the bit at position (xbit, ybit) in "bstring" is "on" (i.e., it has the value 1), it returns **false** otherwise. "bitison" takes 2 arguments: the x and y position of the bit in a 2 dimensional coordinate system. It relies on the two global variables "bstring"

(continued)

```
/bytevalue bstring ybit bwidth mul xbit 8 idiv
    add get def

/mask 1 7 xbit 8 mod sub bitshift def
bytevalue mask and 0 ne
  } def
end

/bitpatternspotfunction
  { setpatterndict begin
    /y exch def /x exch def




    /xindex x 1 add 2 div bpside mul cvi def
    /yindex y 1 add 2 div bpside mul cvi def


    xindex yindex bitison
      { /onbits onbits 1 add def 1 }
      { /offbits offbits 1 add def 0 }
      ifelse
    end
  } def

/setpattern
  { setpatterndict begin
    /cellsz exch def
    /angle exch def
    /bwidth exch def
    /bpside exch def
    /bstring exch def




    /onbits 0 def /offbits 0 def
    cellsz angle /bitpatternspotfunction load
      setuserscreen
    {} settransfer
```

and "bwidth" (documented in "setpattern" below).
Get the integer representation of the hexadecimal
character pair containing the bit to be tested in the
string.
Create a mask to address the correct bit.
Leave the boolean result on the operand stack.

"bitpatternspotfunction" is the procedure provided to
the "setuserscreen" procedure as the spot function.
Like all **setscreen** spot functions, it takes two
arguments: the x and y coordinates of a pixel in a
halftone screen cell. (See the section on Halftone
Screens in the "POSTSCRIPT Language Reference
Manual.") Note that the global variables "onbits" and
"offbits" must be set to 0 before this spot function is
used with the **setscreen** operator (see "setpattern"
below).
First, transform the (x, y) position into a position to
address into the bit pattern. Since the x and y values
provided to the spot function are between -1 and 1,
transform them into integers between 0 and (bpside-1).

If the bit is on, increment the "onbits" count and return
a high value, otherwise increment the "offbits" count
and return a low value.

"setpattern" sets up the halftone screen machinery so
that a repeating bitmap pattern will be used for
subsequent graphics output operations. It takes 5
arguments: "bstring" is the bit pattern represented as a
string, "bpside" is the number of bits per side (the
pattern must be square), "bwidth" is an integer
specifying the width of the pattern in bytes (each row of
the pattern is expressed in an integral number of bytes,
which may contain extra zeroes if "bpside" is not a
multiple of 8), "angle" is the screen angle and "cellsz"
is the halftone screen cell size. The first 3 arguments
later serve as global variables to "bitison."
Initialize "onbits" and "offbits."
Set up the halftone screen.

Don't allow correction of gray values, because we want

(continued)

to set the gray exactly according to the off-bit/total-bits ratio.

By setting the gray this way, the exact number of "on" bits will turn on in the screen. The values of "offbits" and "onbits" are calculated when the **setscreen** operator is executed (see "bitpatternspotfunction" above).

```
          offbits offbits onbits add div setgray
        end
      } def
```

"enlargebits" is used to print an enlarged bit pattern to illustrate the bit patterns used in "setpattern" below. It takes 3 arguments: "bstring," "bpside," and "bwidth" (See description of "setpattern" above). A black square is printed for each "on" bit. The squares are one unit in size so the coordinate system should be scaled appropriately before "enlargebits" is called. Note that the earlier bits in the pattern are printed in the lower positions of the grid. The high order bit of the first byte of the pattern is the lower left bit, and the low order bit of the last byte in the pattern is the upper right bit.

```
/enlargebits
  { /bwidth exch def
    /bpside exch def
    /bstring exch def
```

```
    0.08 setlinewidth
    0 1 bpside 1 sub
      { /y exch def
        0 1 bpside 1 sub
          { /x exch def
            x y setpatterndict /bitison get cvx exec
              { gsave
                  x y translate
                  newpath
                    0 0 moveto 0 1 lineto
                    1 1 lineto 1 0 lineto
                  closepath
                  gsave 0 setgray fill grestore
                  1 setgray stroke
                grestore
              } if
          } for
      } for
    newpath
      0 0 moveto  0 bpside lineto
      bpside dup lineto  bpside 0 lineto
    closepath 0 setgray stroke
  } def
```

Specify a small line width since this will be scaled.
For each bit in the y direction ...

For each bit in the x direction ...

If the bit is "on" print a black square at the appropriate place on the page.

Define a 1 unit square path.

Fill it in with black.
Put a white outline around it.

Put a black outline around the entire bit pattern.

(continued)

```
/inch {72 mul} def

/showpattern
  { /ang exch def
   /pat exch def
   gsave
     0 3.5 inch translate
     3 8 div inch dup scale
     pat 8 1 enlargebits
   grestore
   pat 8 1 ang 72 300 32 div div setpattern



   newpath
     0 0 moveto 3 inch 0 lineto
     3 inch dup lineto 0 3 inch lineto
   closepath fill
  } def

/pat1 <d1e3c5885c3e1d88> def
/pat2 <3e418080e3140808> def


/Helvetica findfont 12 scalefont setfont

gsave
  1 inch 1.25 inch translate
  pat1 0 showpattern
grestore
1 inch 1 inch moveto
(Basket weave, no rotation in user space) show

gsave
  4.5 inch 1.25 inch translate
  pat2 90 showpattern
grestore
4.5 inch 1 inch moveto
(Fish scale, 90 degree rotation) show
( in user space) show
showpage
```

''showpattern'' demonstrates the use of the above functions. First display a pattern as enlarged bits, and then use it to fill an area below the enlarged bits on the page.

Show the enlarged version of the pattern.

First set up the pattern with the halftone screen machinery. The patterns we are using are 8 bits wide (i.e., 1 byte wide) and we want a target frequency that is a multiple of 16 bits (see implementation note above). Define an area to be filled.

Use hexadecimal string notation to set the bit patterns. Each pair of hexadecimal characters represents a ''row'' in the bit pattern.

Font used for printing captions.

Show a basket weave pattern on the left.

Show a fish scale pattern on the right, but rotate it by 90 degrees. The enlarged bitmap pattern is not rotated but the filled area is.

outline OUTLINE
outline OUTLINE

Making an Outline Font

Re-encoding an Entire Font

Boktryckarkonsten är källan till praktiskt taget all mänsklig odling.
Printing is the source of practically all human evolution.
Den förutan hade de oerhörda framstegen inom vetenskap
Without it the tremendous progress in the fields of science and
och teknik inte varit möjliga.
technology would not have been possible.
–VALTER FALK

Making Small Changes
to Encoding Vectors

Changing the Character Widths
of a Font

•Every bullet has its billet. –William III
•The bullet that will kill me is not yet cast. –Napoleon I
•The ballot is stronger than the bullet. –Abraham Lincoln

•Every bullet has its billet. –William III
•The bullet that will kill me is not yet cast. –Napoleon I
•The ballot is stronger than the bullet. –Abraham Lincoln

•Every bullet has its billet. –William III
•The bullet that will kill me is not yet cast. –Napoleon I
•The ballot is stronger than the bullet. –Abraham Lincoln

Hieroglyphics are the root of letters. All
characters were originally signs and all
signs were once images. Human society,
the world, man in his entirety is in the
alphabet.□

Creating an Analytic Font

the tendency of the best
typography has been and
still should be in the path of
simplicity, legibility, and
orderly arrangement.

Creating a Bitmap Font

MODIFYING AND CREATING FONTS

Although a large variety of fonts are available with the POSTSCRIPT language, there are situations when users may wish to modify the existing fonts or create new fonts. This section presents several examples of modifying existing fonts to change their rendering style (from filled to outlined), the character widths or the encoding of characters. There are also 2 examples of creating entirely new fonts: one using bitmap character descriptions and the other using analytic character descriptions.

The basic underlying structure of a font is the *font dictionary*. When fonts are modified, the entries in the font dictionary are changed. When new fonts are created, certain crucial entries in the font dictionary must be present. Some of the details on the entries in a font dictionary and how to modify them are explained below; for a full explanation refer to the *POSTSCRIPT Language Reference Manual*.

MODIFYING EXISTING FONTS

The basic strategy for modifying an existing font is to create an entirely new font dictionary and to copy all the references to entries in the original font dictionary, except for the FID entry, into the new dictionary. The next step is to modify the appropriate fields. The last step is to perform a **definefont** operation on the modified font dictionary to make it into a POSTSCRIPT font.

There are two important steps to remember when modifying an existing font. The first is *not* to copy the FID field from the original font dictionary to the new dictionary. The FID field will automatically get created when the **definefont** operator is executed. Attempting to perform a **definefont** operation on a dictionary that already contains an FID field results in an **invalidfont** error. The second step is to change the FontName field in the new dictionary. The same name which appears in the FontName field should be provided as an argument to the **definefont** operator. *The FontName should always be a unique name.*

In addition, for fonts that have a UniqueID field, it is important to change the UniqueID field when the font is modified. The only case when the UniqueID field should *not* be changed is when the Encoding field of a font dictionary has been changed. Changing the UniqueID should be done with care. See the programs ''Making an Outline Font'' and ''Changing the Character Widths of a Font'' for examples of this.

CREATING NEW FONTS

When creating new fonts, certain font dictionary entries *must* be present. They are FontMatrix, FontType, FontBBox, Encoding and BuildChar. For a user defined font, the FontType should always have the value 3. In addition, it is useful, although not necessary, to have a UniqueID entry. The UniqueID entry facilitates better caching of characters on disk-based implementations of the POSTSCRIPT interpreter. (Be forewarned that the UniqueID must truly be a unique 24 bit number and that the creator of the font is responsible for ensuring this.)

The BuildChar procedure is responsible for specifying how a character in the new font is rendered. It should always call either the **setcachedevice** or **setcharwidth** operator. The BuildChar procedure can use almost all of the POSTSCRIPT operators to render a character. However, there are some restrictions when the character is to be cached (i.e., when the **setcachedevice** operator has been used). In this case, any of the operators related to gray-level and color are invalid (e.g., **setgray**, **setrgbcolor**, **image**, etc).

In the character descriptions for a new font, it is a good idea to create a character description that will be printed for "undefined" characters. This character is called ".notdef" in the built-in fonts, and it is defined to print nothing. When users try to print characters that have not been defined in the font, the ".notdef" character is printed; the ".notdef" character is a graceful way of avoiding unexpected errors. As well as creating a character description for the undefined character, it is important that the encoding vector have the name of this undefined character in each location that does not have a character defined. The simplest way to do this is to initialize all the entries in the encoding vector to contain the ".notdef" character and then enter the character names in the desired positions.

ABOUT THE PROGRAMS

The program "Making an Outline Font" is an example of modifying an existing font to change its rendering style. The program defines a general procedure "MakeOutlineFont" that takes one of the standard built-in fonts and converts it to an outline font. (The term "built-in fonts" refers to the collection of fonts available with a POSTSCRIPT implementation.) This procedure will only yield the correct results for fonts that have their characters described as outlines.

"Re-encoding an Entire Font" presents a general procedure "ReEncode" for changing the encoding vector of a font. The encoding vector is a mapping of character codes (in the range of 0 to 255) to character names. Most of the built-in fonts are encoded according to a standard encoding, but there are cases where other encodings may be required such as printing text that has been represented according to the EBCDIC encoding. The specific example demonstrated in the program "Re-encoding an Entire Font" re-encodes a built-in font to have the EBCDIC encoding by replacing the encoding vector in the font dictionary with an entirely new encoding vector.

"Making Small Changes to Encoding Vectors" presents an alternative to replacing the entire encoding vector for situations when the encoding vector only needs to be changed slightly. Most of the built-in fonts contain characters that have not been encoded, such as accented characters. To print such characters, the name of the character must be inserted into the encoding vector. However, we do not want to specify the entire encoding vector to insert a few new characters so the procedure ''ReEncodeSmall'' has been defined to handle this insertion.

When encoding accented characters it is important to understand that accented characters (also known as *composite characters*) are actually a composite of the letter and the accent. In order to print accented characters properly, both the letter and the accent of the composite character must be encoded in the encoding vector, as well as the composite character itself. For example, if you wish to encode the composite character ''Aacute,'' both the ''A'' and the ''acute'' must be encoded.

''Changing the Character Widths of a Font'' defines a general procedure, ''ModifyWidths,'' for changing some or all of the character widths in a given font. It changes the necessary entries in the font dictionary. In this example the character widths of a font are rounded such that when the characters are printed at a certain point size, the widths will be an integral number of pixels in device space. This is useful for avoiding round-off error in positioning characters with the **show** operator.

The program ''Creating an Analytic Font'' demonstrates how to create a new font whose character descriptions are geometric in nature. The program defines all the necessary font dictionary entries as well as some new entries of its own. The font created has 4 characters: bullets of three sizes and an open box shape. Each character is described using the POSTSCRIPT graphic operators. After the font has been defined it is used in an example that prints the various characters intermixed with one of the built-in fonts.

The final program, ''Creating a Bitmap Font,'' demonstrates an efficient way to create a new font whose character descriptions are bitmaps.

Making an Outline Font

Re-encoding an Entire Font

Boktryckarkonsten är källan till praktiskt taget all mänsklig odling.
Printing is the source of practically all human evolution.
Den förutan hade de oerhörda framstegen inom vetenskap
Without it the tremendous progress in the fields of science and
och teknik inte varit möjliga.
technology would not have been possible.
—VALTER FALK

Making Small Changes
to Encoding Vectors

Changing the Character Widths
of a Font

•Every bullet has its billet. –William III
•The bullet that will kill me is not yet cast. –Napoleon I
•The ballot is stronger than the bullet. –Abraham Lincoln

•Every bullet has its billet. –William III
•The bullet that will kill me is not yet cast. –Napoleon I
•The ballot is stronger than the bullet. –Abraham Lincoln

•Every bullet has its billet. –William III
•The bullet that will kill me is not yet cast. –Napoleon I
•The ballot is stronger than the bullet. –Abraham Lincoln

Hieroglyphics are the root of letters. All
characters were originally signs and all
signs were once images. Human society,
the world, man in his entirety is in the
alphabet.□

Creating an Analytic Font

the tendency of the best
typography has been and
still should be in the path of
simplicity, legibility, and
orderly arrangement.

Theodore low de dinne

Creating a Bitmap Font

outlineoutline
outlineoutline

1 inch
72 points

This program defines a general procedure to take one of the built-in filled fonts and convert it into an outline font. (This program will also work for downloadable fonts available from Adobe Systems, Inc.).

```
/makeoutlinedict 7 dict def
/MakeOutlineFont
  { makeoutlinedict begin
   /uniqueid exch def
   /strokewidth exch def
   /newfontname exch def
   /basefontname exch def
```

Local storage for the procedure "MakeOutlineFont." "MakeOutlineFont" takes one of the built-in filled fonts and makes an outlined font out of it. It takes four arguments: the name of the font on which to base the outline version, the new name for the outline font, a stroke width to use on the outline and a unique ID.

```
   /basefontdict basefontname findfont def
```

Get the dictionary of the font on which the outline version will be based.

```
   /numentries basefontdict maxlength 1 add def
```

Determine how large the new font dictionary for the outline font should be. Make it one entry larger to accommodate an entry for the stroke width used on the outline.

```
   basefontdict /UniqueID known not
    { /numentries numentries 1 add def } if
```

Make sure there is room for the unique ID field. (Not all fonts have UniqueID fields initially. In particular, the built-in fonts in POSTSCRIPT version 23.0 do not.)

```
   /outfontdict numentries dict def
```

Create a dictionary to hold the description for the outline font.

```
   basefontdict
    { exch dup /FID ne
      { exch outfontdict 3 1 roll put }
      { pop pop }
      ifelse
    } forall
```

Copy all the entries in the base font dictionary to the outline dictionary, except for the FID.

Ignore the FID pair.

```
   outfontdict /FontName newfontname put
   outfontdict /PaintType 2 put
   outfontdict /StrokeWidth strokewidth put
   outfontdict /UniqueID uniqueid put
```

Insert the new name into the dictionary.
Change the paint type to outline.
Insert the stroke width into the dictionary.
Insert the new unique ID.

```
   newfontname outfontdict definefont pop
  end
  } def
```

Now make the outline dictionary into a POSTSCRIPT font. We will ignore the modified dictionary returned on the stack by the **definefont** operator.

outlineoutline
outlineoutline

1 inch
72 points

(continued)

The following demonstrates how to use the ''MakeOutlineFont'' procedure and how to determine new unique ID's.

```
/Helvetica-Bold /Helvetica-Outline1 1000 54 div
```

The stroke width is always specified in the character coordinate system (1000 units) The value specified here, 1000/54 will yield a one point wide outline when the font is scaled to 54 points in size. Note that this outline width changes with different point sizes.

```
/Helvetica-Bold findfont dup /UniqueID known
  { /UniqueID get 1 add }
  { pop 1 }
  ifelse
MakeOutlineFont
```

Determine the unique ID. If the ''base'' font already contains a unique ID, add a unique constant to it, otherwise pick a unique integer and leave that value on the operand stack.

```
/Helvetica-Outline1 findfont 36 scalefont setfont
  72 504 moveto (outline) show
```

```
/Helvetica-Outline1 findfont 54 scalefont setfont
  (outline) show
```

```
/Helvetica-Bold /Helvetica-Outline2 1000 36 div
```

A stroke width value of 1000/36 yields a one point wide outline when the font is scaled to 36 points in size. It yields a 1.5 point outline when the font is scaled to 54 points in size (54/36 = 1.5).

```
/Helvetica-Bold findfont dup /UniqueID known
  { /UniqueID get 2 add }
  { pop 2 }
  ifelse
MakeOutlineFont
```

```
/Helvetica-Outline2 findfont 36 scalefont setfont
  72 444 moveto (outline) show
```

```
/Helvetica-Outline2 findfont 54 scalefont setfont
  (outline) show
showpage
```

NOTE: If the font is scaled anamorphically, the outline stroke on the characters will be scaled anamorphically as well, leading to potentially undesirable results.

Octal Number	Standard Char	EBCDIC Char	Octal Number	Standard Char	EBCDIC Char	Octal Number	Standard Char	EBCDIC Char	Octal Number	Standard Char	EBCDIC Char
0			100	@		200			300		
1			101	A		201		a	301	`	A
2			102	B		202		b	302	´	B
3			103	C		203		c	303	^	C
4			104	D		204		d	304	~	D
5			105	E		205		e	305	¯	E
6			106	F		206		f	306	˘	F
7			107	G		207		g	307	˙	G
10			110	H		210		h	310	¨	H
11			111	I		211		i	311		I
12			112	J	¢	212			312	°	
13			113	K	.	213			313		
14			114	L	<	214			314	¸	
15			115	M	(	215			315	˝	
16			116	N	+	216			316		
17			117	O	|	217			317	ˇ	
20			120	P	&	220			320	—	
21			121	Q		221		j	321		J
22			122	R		222		k	322		K
23			123	S		223		l	323		L
24			124	T		224		m	324		M
25			125	U		225		n	325		N
26			126	V		226		o	326		O
27			127	W		227		p	327		P
30			130	X		230		q	330		Q
31			131	Y		231		r	331		R
32			132	Z	!	232			332		
33			133	[	$	233			333		
34			134	\	*	234			334		
35			135	]	)	235			335		
36			136	^	;	236			336		
37			137	_	~	237			337		
40			140	`	-	240			340		
41	!		141	a	/	241	¡		341	Æ	
42	"		142	b		242	¢	s	342		S
43	#		143	c		243	£	t	343	ª	T
44	$		144	d		244	⁄	u	344		U
45	%		145	e		245	¥	v	345		V
46	&		146	f		246	ƒ	w	346		W
47	'		147	g		247	§	x	347		X
50	(		150	h		250	¤	y	350	Ł	Y
51	)		151	i		251	'	z	351	Ø	Z
52	*		152	j		252	"		352	Œ	
53	+		153	k	,	253	«		353	º	
54	,		154	l	%	254	‹		354		
55	-		155	m	_	255	›		355		
56	.		156	n	>	256	fi		356		
57	/		157	o	?	257	fl		357		
60	0		160	p		260			360		0
61	1		161	q		261	–		361	æ	1
62	2		162	r		262	†		362		2
63	3		163	s		263	‡		363		3
64	4		164	t		264	·		364		4
65	5		165	u		265			365	ı	5
66	6		166	v		266	¶		366		6
67	7		167	w		267	•		367		7
70	8		170	x		270	‚		370	ł	8
71	9		171	y		271	„		371	ø	9
72	:		172	z	:	272	"		372	œ	
73	;		173	{	#	273	»		373	ß	
74	<		174	|	@	274	…		374		
75	=		175	}	'	275	‰		375		
76	>		176	~	=	276			376		
77	?		177		"	277	¿		377		

1 inch

72 points

This program defines a general procedure for re-encoding the entire encoding vector for a font. The specific example demonstrated shows how to re-encode one of the built-in fonts according to the EBCDIC character set encoding.

```
/reencodedict 5 dict def
/ReEncode
  { reencodedict begin
    /newencoding exch def
    /newfontname exch def
    /basefontname exch def
```

Local storage for the procedure "ReEncode."
"ReEncode" generates a new re-encoded font. It takes 3 arguments: the name of the font to be re-encoded, a new name, and a new encoding vector. ReEncode copies the existing font dictionary, replacing the FontName and Encoding fields, then generates a new FID and enters the new name in FontDirectory with the **definefont** operator. The new name provided can later be used in a **findfont** operation.

```
    /basefontdict basefontname findfont def
```

Get the dictionary of the font on which the re-encoded version will be based.

```
    /newfont basefontdict maxlength dict def
```

Create a dictionary to hold the description for the re-encoded font.

```
    basefontdict
    { exch dup dup /FID ne exch /Encoding ne and
      { exch newfont 3 1 roll put }
      { pop pop }
      ifelse
    } forall
```

Copy all the entries in the base font dictionary to the new dictionary except for the FID and Encoding fields.

Ignore the FID and Encoding pairs.

```
    newfont /FontName newfontname put
    newfont /Encoding newencoding put
```

Install the new name and the new encoding vector in the font.

```
    newfontname newfont definefont pop
  end
} def
```

Now make the re-encoded font dictionary into a POSTSCRIPT font. Ignore the modified dictionary on the operand stack returned by the **definefont** operator.

```
/EBCDIC 256 array def
0 1 255 { EBCDIC exch /.notdef put } for
EBCDIC
  dup 8#100 /space put
  dup 8#112 /cent put    dup 8#116 /plus put
  dup 8#113 /period put dup 8#117 /bar put
  dup 8#114 /less put    dup 8#120 /ampersand put
  dup 8#115 /parenleft put

  dup 8#132 /exclam put   dup 8#140 /hyphen put
  dup 8#133 /dollar put    dup 8#141 /slash put
  dup 8#134 /asterisk put
  dup 8#135 /parenright put
  dup 8#136 /semicolon put
  dup 8#137 /asciitilde put
```

To illustrate how the ReEncode procedure is used, we will re-encode one of the built-in fonts to support the EBCDIC encoding. (The EBCDIC encoding used is referenced in "IBM System/360: Principles of Operation," Appendix F.) The first step in doing this is to define an array containing that encoding. This array is referred to as an "encoding vector." The encoding vector should be 256 entries long. Since the encoding vector is rather sparse, all the entries are initialized to ".notdef." Those entries which correspond to characters in the EBCDIC encoding are filled in with the proper character name. The octal character code for the character is used to access the encoding vector.

(continued)

dup 8#153 /comma put
dup 8#154 /percent put
dup 8#155 /underscore put
dup 8#156 /greater put
dup 8#157 /question put

dup 8#172 /colon put
dup 8#173 /numbersign put
dup 8#174 /at put
dup 8#175 /quoteright put
dup 8#176 /equal put
dup 8#177 /quotedbl put

dup 8#201 /a put   dup 8#206 /f put
dup 8#202 /b put   dup 8#207 /g put
dup 8#203 /c put   dup 8#210 /h put
dup 8#204 /d put   dup 8#211 /i put
dup 8#205 /e put

dup 8#221 /j put   dup 8#226 /o put
dup 8#222 /k put   dup 8#227 /p put
dup 8#223 /l put   dup 8#230 /q put
dup 8#224 /m put   dup 8#231 /r put
dup 8#225 /n put

dup 8#242 /s put   dup 8#246 /w put
dup 8#243 /t put   dup 8#247 /x put
dup 8#244 /u put   dup 8#250 /y put
dup 8#245 /v put   dup 8#251 /z put

dup 8#301 /A put   dup 8#306 /F put
dup 8#302 /B put   dup 8#307 /G put
dup 8#303 /C put   dup 8#310 /H put
dup 8#304 /D put   dup 8#311 /I put
dup 8#305 /E put

dup 8#321 /J put   dup 8#326 /O put
dup 8#322 /K put   dup 8#327 /P put
dup 8#323 /L put   dup 8#330 /Q put
dup 8#324 /M put   dup 8#331 /R put
dup 8#325 /N put

dup 8#342 /S put   dup 8#346 /W put
dup 8#343 /T put   dup 8#347 /X put
dup 8#344 /U put   dup 8#350 /Y put
dup 8#345 /V put   dup 8#351 /Z put

Continuation of the EBCDIC encoding vector
definition.

(continued)

```
dup 8#360 /zero put   dup 8#365 /five put
dup 8#361 /one put    dup 8#366 /six put
dup 8#362 /two put    dup 8#367 /seven put
dup 8#363 /three put  dup 8#370 /eight put
dup 8#364 /four put   dup 8#371 /nine put
pop
```
Remove the array from the operand stack.

```
/TR /Times-Roman findfont 10 scalefont def
/Times-Roman /Times-Roman-EBCDIC EBCDIC
  ReEncode
/TRE /Times-Roman-EBCDIC findfont 10 scalefont
 def
```
Print a table comparing the standard POSTSCRIPT character set encoding with the EBCDIC encoding. Set up the fonts to be used: Times Roman with the standard encoding and Times Roman with the EBCDIC encoding.

```
TR setfont
0 1 3
  { /counter exch def
    40 counter 133 mul add 720 moveto
    ( Octal    Standard    EBCDIC) show
    40 counter 133 mul add 720 10 sub moveto
    (Number    Char        Char) show
  } for
```
Print each column heading in the standard Times Roman.

```
/showstring 1 string def
/counterstring 3 string def
```
String definitions used to show characters and numbers below.

```
/yline 690 def
/xstart 52 def
0 1 255
  { /counter exch def
    /charstring showstring dup 0 counter put def
    TR setfont  xstart yline moveto
    counter 8 counterstring cvrs show
    xstart 42 add yline moveto
    charstring show
    TRE setfont  xstart 86 add yline moveto
    charstring show
    /yline yline 10 sub def
    counter 1 add 64 mod 0 eq
      { /xstart xstart 133 add def
        /yline 690 def
      } if
  } for
```
Print the table of character codes and corresponding characters.
For each character code from 0 to 255, print the corresponding standard and EBCDIC characters.

Print the character code in octal using **cvrs.**

Print the corresponding standard character.

Print the corresponding EBCDIC character.
Move down one line.
If we have reached the 64th line, move over by a column and start at the top again.

```
showpage
```

Boktryckarkonsten är källan till praktiskt taget all mänsklig odling.
Printing is the source of practically all human evolution.
Den förutan hade de oerhörda framstegen inom vetenskap
Without it the tremendous progress in the fields of science and
och teknik inte varit möjliga.
technology would not have been possible.
–VALTER FALK

This program is slightly different from the previous program in that it keeps the original encoding vector of the font but it overwrites portions of it with the new encodings specified. This method is useful when re-encoding a font to contain accented (composite) characters.

```
/reencsmalldict 12 dict def
/ReEncodeSmall
  { reencsmalldict begin
  /newcodesandnames exch def
  /newfontname exch def
  /basefontname exch def
```

Local storage for the procedure ''ReEncodeSmall.'' ''ReEncodeSmall'' generates a new re-encoded font. It takes 3 arguments: the name of the font to be re-encoded, a new name, and an array of new character encoding and character name pairs (see the definition of the ''scandvec'' array below for the format of this array). This method has the advantage that it allows the user to make changes to an existing encoding vector without having to specify an entire new encoding vector. It also saves space when the character encoding and name pairs array is smaller than an entire encoding vector.

```
/basefontdict basefontname findfont def
```

Get the font dictionary on which to base the re-encoded version.

```
/newfont basefontdict maxlength dict def
```

Create a dictionary to hold the description for the re-encoded font.

```
basefontdict
  { exch dup /FID ne
    { dup /Encoding eq
      { exch dup length array copy
        newfont 3 1 roll put }
      { exch newfont 3 1 roll put }
      ifelse
    }
    { pop pop }
    ifelse
  } forall
```

Copy all the entries in the base font dictionary to the new dictionary except for the FID field.

Make a copy of the Encoding field.

Ignore the FID pair.

```
newfont /FontName newfontname put
newcodesandnames aload pop
```

Install the new name.
Modify the encoding vector. First load the new encoding and name pairs onto the operand stack.

```
newcodesandnames length 2 idiv
  { newfont /Encoding get 3 1 roll put}
  repeat
```

For each pair on the stack, put the new name into the designated position in the encoding vector.

```
newfontname newfont definefont pop
end
} def
```

Now make the re-encoded font description into a POSTSCRIPT font. Ignore the modified dictionary returned on the operand stack by the **definefont** operator.

Boktryckarkonsten är källan till praktiskt taget all mänsklig odling.
Printing is the source of practically all human evolution.
Den förutan hade de oerhörda framstegen inom vetenskap
Without it the tremendous progress in the fields of science and
och teknik inte varit möjliga.
technology would not have been possible.
–VALTER FALK

```
/scandvec [
  8#300 /Oacute
  8#311 /Adieresis
  8#321 /oacute
  8#322 /Ograve
  8#323 /Scaron
  8#324 /ograve
  8#325 /scaron
  8#330 /Edieresis
  8#331 /adieresis
  8#332 /edieresis
  8#333 /Odieresis
  8#334 /odieresis
  8#340 /Aacute
  8#342 /Aring
  8#344 /Zcaron
  8#347 /Eacute
  8#360 /aacute
  8#362 /aring
  8#364 /zcaron
  8#367 /eacute
  ] def
```

Define an array of new character encoding and name pairs that will enable us to print the accented characters in the Scandinavian languages. The array is a series of encoding number and name pairs. The encoding number always precedes the character name. Since it contains pairs, there must be an even number of elements in this array. The encoding vector positions for these new characters have been chosen so that they do not actually replace any of the characters in the standard encoding.

```
/ss { 72 yline moveto show
      /yline yline 36 sub def } def
```

This procedure shows a string and then skips a line.

```
/Times-Roman /Times-Roman-Scand scandvec
  ReEncodeSmall
/Times-Roman-Scand findfont 16 scalefont
  setfont
/yline 500 def
(Boktryckarkonsten \331r k\331llan till praktiskt\
 taget all m\331nsklig odling.) ss
(Den f\334rutan hade de oerh\334rda framstegen\
 inom vetenskap) ss
(och teknik inte varit m\334jliga.) ss
(\261VALTER FALK) ss

/Times-Italic findfont 14 scalefont setfont
/yline 500 18 sub def
(Printing is the source of practically all human\
 evolution.) ss
(Without it the tremendous progress in the\
 fields of science and) ss
(technology would not have been possible.) ss
showpage
```

Re-encode the standard Times Roman to include the accented characters for the Scandinavian Languages. Print some text with accented characters. Since the accented characters are in the upper half of the encoding vector we must refer to them by their octal codes.

6 point   HOHOHOHO oaobocodoeofogohoiojokolomonopoqorosotouovowoxoyoz
           HOHOHOHO oaobocodoeofogohoiojokolomonopoqorosotouovowoxoyoz

7 point   HOHOHOHO oaobocodoeofogohoiojokolomonopoqorosotouovowoxoyoz
           HOHOHOHO oaobocodoeofogohoiojokolomonopoqorosotouovowoxoyoz

8 point   HOHOHOHO oaobocodoeofogohoiojokolomonopoqorosotouovowoxoyoz
           HOHOHOHO oaobocodoeofogohoiojokolomonopoqorosotouovowoxoyoz

Although the program to the right is device independent, this page was printed on a 300 dot per inch printer to emphasize the effect of rounding character widths.

This program demonstrates how to change the character widths of a font. The specific example used shows how to round the character widths such that when the font is printed at a certain point size, the widths are an integral number of pixels in device space.

```
/modwidthsdict 8 dict def
/ModifyWidths
  { modwidthsdict begin
    /uniqueid exch def
    /newwidths exch def
    /newfontname exch def
    /basefontname exch def
    /basefontdict basefontname findfont def


    /numentries basefontdict maxlength 1 add def


    basefontdict /UniqueID known not
      { /numentries numentries 1 add def } if
    /newfont numentries dict def
    basefontdict
    { exch dup dup /FID ne exch
      /FontBBox ne and
      { exch newfont 3 1 roll put }
      { pop pop }
      ifelse
    } forall
    /newFontBBox basefontdict /FontBBox get
      aload length array astore def




    newfont /FontBBox newFontBBox put
    newfont /FontName newfontname put
    newfont /Metrics newwidths put
    newfont /UniqueID uniqueid put
    newfontname newfont definefont pop
  end
} def
```

Local storage for the procedure ''ModifyWidths.'' ''ModifyWidths'' generates a new font. It takes 4 arguments: the name of the font whose widths are to be changed, a new name, a dictionary containing the new widths and a unique ID. ModifyWidths copies the existing font dictionary, replacing the FontName field, adds a Metrics entry and then defines a new font.
Get the dictionary of the font on which the new version will be based.
Determine how large the new font dictionary should be. Make sure it is one entry larger than the previous one so that it has room for the Metrics entry.
Make sure there is room for the UniqueID field.

Create the new dictionary
Copy all the entries in the base font dictionary to the new dictionary except for the FID and FontBBox (see explanation below) fields.

Ignore the FID and FontBBox pairs.

Due to a problem in POSTSCRIPT version 23.0 it is necessary to create an entirely new FontBBox entry rather than simply make a copy. A new array is created that contains the same values for the font bounding box as the base font has.
Install the new font bounding box.
Install the new name and widths in the font.

Install the new unique ID.
Now make the font dictionary with the new metrics into a POSTSCRIPT font. Ignore the dictionary returned on the operand stack by the **definefont** operator.

(continued)

```
/roundwidthsdict 13 dict def
```
Local storage for the procedure "roundwidths."

```
roundwidthsdict /showstring 1 string put
```
String used for **stringwidth** operations.

```
/roundwidths
  { roundwidthsdict begin
   /ptsize exch def
   /resolution exch def
   /fontname exch def
```
"roundwidths" takes three arguments: a POSTSCRIPT font name, a point size, and the resolution of the output device (in the x direction). The resolution is specified in pixels per inch. "roundwidths" returns a dictionary of rounded widths on the operand stack. The widths are rounded so that when they are scaled to the specified point size, they will be an integral number of pixels in device space.

```
   /thefont fontname findfont def
   /newwidths thefont /CharStrings get length
     dict def
```
Get the font dictionary associated with the font name. Allocate a new dictionary for widths. Make it as large as necessary (there will never be more widths than there are CharStrings entries).

```
   /pixelsperem ptsize 72 div resolution mul def
```
Determine how many pixels are required for the given point size.

```
   /unitsperpixel 1000 pixelsperem div def
```
Determine how many units (in the 1000 unit font space) map to one pixel.

```
   gsave
    nulldevice
```
Perform the width calculations under the null device so that we will get the actual widths without rounding effects from the output device.

```
    thefont 1 scalefont setfont
```
Use a 1 unit high font; it speeds up the time required for determining the width of characters.

```
   /charcount 0 def
   thefont /Encoding get
     { /charname exch def
      charname /.notdef ne
```
Compute the current width for each character in the encoding vector.

```
       { /charwidth showstring dup 0 charcount
         put stringwidth pop 1000 mul def
        /multiples charwidth unitsperpixel div
          round cvi def
        /newcharwidth unitsperpixel multiples
          mul def
```
Get the current character width by performing a **stringwidth** operation and convert it to 1000ths.

```
        newwidths charname newcharwidth put
       } if
      /charcount charcount 1 add def
     } forall
   grestore
   newwidths
   end
  } def
```
Store the newly computed width in the new dictionary of widths.

Leave the new dictionary of widths on the operand stack.

(continued)

```
/findresdict 4 dict def
findresdict begin
  /tempmatrix matrix def
  /epsilon 0.001 def
end
```

Local storage for the procedure "findresolution."

Matrix used in computations.
Error tolerance (see the "findresolution" procedure below).

```
/findresolution
  { findresdict begin
      72 0 tempmatrix defaultmatrix dtransform
      /y exch def /x exch def

      x abs epsilon gt y abs epsilon gt and
      { stop }

      { x dup mul y dup mul add sqrt }
      ifelse
    end
  } def
```

"findresolution" returns the resolution (in pixels per inch) in the x-direction of the device being printed on. Since there are 72 units per inch in the default user space, find out how many pixels those 72 units require in device space.
If both the x and y components of the vector returned by the **dtransform** are larger than the error tolerance, refuse to continue because we are in some non-90 degree rotated device space that wouldn't make any sense in our computations.
Leave the x-resolution on the operand stack.

The following prints a comparison of rounded vs. non-rounded widths.

```
/showstring
  { (HOHOHOHO oₐobocodoeofogohoiojoko) show
    (lomonopoqorosotouovowoxoyoz) show } def
/res findresolution
/uid /Times-Roman findfont dup /UniqueID known
  {/UniqueID get}{pop 0} ifelse def
/rwid /Times-Roman res 6 roundwidths def
/Times-Roman /TR6 rwid uid 1 add ModifyWidths
/Times-Roman findfont 6 scalefont setfont
130 560 moveto showstring
/TR6 findfont 6 scalefont setfont
130 560 6 sub moveto showstring
/rwid /Times-Roman res 7 roundwidths def
/Times-Roman /TR7 rwid uid 2 add ModifyWidths
/Times-Roman findfont 7 scalefont setfont
130 500 moveto showstring
/TR7 findfont 7 scalefont setfont
130 500 7 sub moveto showstring
/rwid /Times-Roman res 8 roundwidths def
/Times-Roman /TR8 rwid uid 3 add ModifyWidths
/Times-Roman findfont 8 scalefont setfont
130 440 moveto showstring
/TR8 findfont 8 scalefont setfont
130 440 8 sub moveto showstring
showpage
```

This procedure simply shows a string of text.

Get the resolution of the printing device.
Find the original unique ID for the font we are using. If it doesn't have a unique ID, use zero.
Compute the rounded widths for 6 pt. Times Roman.
Create a new font with the 6 pt. rounded widths.
Print the normal 6 pt. Times Roman.

Print the 6 pt. Times Roman with rounded widths.

Repeat the same procedure for 7 point Times Roman.

Repeat the same procedure for 8 point Times Roman.

•Every bullet has its billet. –William III
•The bullet that will kill me is not yet cast. –Napoleon I
•The ballot is stronger than the bullet. –Abraham Lincoln

•Every bullet has its billet. –William III
•The bullet that will kill me is not yet cast. –Napoleon I
•The ballot is stronger than the bullet. –Abraham Lincoln

●Every bullet has its billet. –William III
●The bullet that will kill me is not yet cast. –Napoleon I
●The ballot is stronger than the bullet. –Abraham Lincoln

Hieroglyphics are the root of letters. All
characters were originally signs and all
signs were once images. Human society,
the world, man in his entirety is in the
alphabet.□

1 inch
72 points

This program demonstrates how to define an entirely new font with analytic (geometric) character descriptions.

```
10 dict dup begin
```

Create a dictionary for the font. Leave room for the FID (fontID) entry.

```
/FontType 3 def
/FontMatrix [.001 0 0 .001 0 0] def
```

FontType 3 indicates that this is a user defined font. Since the font coordinate system used for this font is based on units of 1000 (as are the built-in fonts), specify a FontMatrix that transforms the 1000 unit system to a 1 unit system.

```
/FontBBox [50 0 760 700] def
```

This is the bounding box that would result if all the characters in the font were overlapped.

```
/Encoding 256 array def
0 1 255 {Encoding exch /.notdef put} for
Encoding
  dup (a) 0 get /smallbullet put
  dup (b) 0 get /mediumbullet put
  dup (c) 0 get /largebullet put
  (d) 0 get /openbox put
```

Allocate storage for the encoding vector.
Initialize all the entries in the encoding vector with ''.notdef''.
Associate the small bullet character with the character code for a lowercase a, associate the medium bullet character with the character code for a lowercase b, and so on.

```
/Metrics 5 dict def
Metrics begin
  /.notdef 0 def
  /smallbullet 400 def
  /mediumbullet 520 def
  /largebullet 640 def
  /openbox 820 def
end
```

Allocate storage for the character widths.

Make sure there is a width for the ''.notdef'' character as well as for all the other characters in the font.

```
/BBox 5 dict def
BBox begin
  /.notdef [0 0 0 0] def
  /smallbullet [50 200 350 500] def
  /mediumbullet [50 150 450 550] def
  /largebullet [50 100 550 600] def
  /openbox [60 0 760 700] def
end
```

Create a dictionary for storing information about the bounding boxes of the character descriptions.
Make sure there is a bounding box for ''.notdef''.

The bounding box for the open box is slightly larger than the path definition because it is stroked. Half of the strokewidth (60/2 =30) is added to bounding box of the outline.

```
/CharacterDefs 5 dict def
CharacterDefs begin
  /.notdef { } def
```

The ''CharacterDefs'' dictionary will hold the descriptions for rendering the characters.
There should always be a description for the undefined character ''.notdef'' which does nothing.

215

```
/smallbullet
  { newpath
    200 350 150 0 360 arc
    closepath
    fill } def
/mediumbullet
  { newpath
    250 350 200 0 360 arc
    closepath
    fill } def
/largebullet
  { newpath
    300 350 250 0 360 arc
    closepath
    fill } def
/openbox
  { newpath
    90 30 moveto    90 670 lineto
    730 670 lineto  730 30 lineto
    closepath
    60 setlinewidth
    stroke } def
end
```

''smallbullet'' defines a path for drawing a small bullet centered in the capheight of a font (in this case capheight=700 units). It also fills the path.

''mediumbullet'' is defined similarly to ''smallbullet.''

''largebullet'' is defined similarly to ''smallbullet.''

''openbox'' defines a path for drawing an outlined box that rests on the baseline and is as tall as the capheight (700 units). It strokes the path with a line whose thickness is 60 units out of 1000.

Finished defining the characters.

```
/BuildChar
  { 0 begin
    /char exch def
    /fontdict exch def
    /charname fontdict /Encoding get char get def
    fontdict begin
      Metrics charname get 0
      BBox charname get aload pop

      setcachedevice

      CharacterDefs charname get exec
    end
  end
  } def
/BuildChar load 0 3 dict put
/UniqueID 1 def
end
```

The procedure ''BuildChar'' is called every time a character from this font must be constructed.
The character code and font dictionary are provided as arguments.
Convert the character code to the corresponding name by looking it up in the encoding vector.

Find the width of the character.
Find the bounding box of the character and push it onto the stack.
Using the **setcachedevice** operator enables the characters from this font to be cached.
Find the procedure for rendering the character and execute it.

Local storage for the procedure ''BuildChar.''
Create a unique identifier for the font.
Done defining the font dictionary.

```
/BoxesAndBullets exch definefont pop
```

Register the font; name it ''BoxesAndBullets.''

```
/bbfont /BoxesAndBullets findfont 16 scalefont def
/textfont /Times-Roman findfont 16 scalefont def
```

The remainder of this program illustrates the use of the analytic font intermixed with one of the standard text fonts.

```
/ss { 72 yline moveto show
    /yline yline 16 sub def } def
```

This procedure shows a string and then gets ready to move down the page by one line.

```
/showbullettext
  { /bulletchar exch def


    bbfont setfont bulletchar ss
    textfont setfont
    (Every bullet has its billet. \261William III) show
    bbfont setfont bulletchar ss
    textfont setfont
    (The bullet that will kill me is not yet cast.) show
    ( \261Napoleon I) show
    bbfont setfont bulletchar ss
    textfont setfont
    (The ballot is stronger than the bullet.) show
    ( \261Abraham Lincoln) show
  } def
```

"showbullettext" enables us to conveniently show the same series of text but with different bullets each time. A string containing the bullet character is passed as an argument.
Show the bullet character in the BoxesAndBullets font.
Switch to the standard text font.
Show the text immediately following the bullet. (Octal character 261 is an endash.)

```
/yline 650 def (a) showbullettext
/yline 550 def (b) showbullettext
/yline 450 def (c) showbullettext
```

Now show three series of statements, each series with a different sized bullet.

```
/yline 300 def
textfont setfont
(Hieroglyphics are the root of letters. All) ss
(characters were originally signs and all) ss
(signs were once images. Human society,) ss
(the world, man in his entirety is in the) ss
(alphabet.) ss
bbfont setfont
(d) show
```

This example shows a common use of the "openbox" character: as the marker at the end of a paragraph.

Place the "openbox" character at the end of the last line.

```
showpage
```

the tendency of the best
typography has been and
still should be in the path of
simplicity, legibility, and
orderly arrangement.

theodore low de vinne

This program demonstrates how to efficiently define an entirely new font with bitmap character descriptions.

```
9 dict dup begin
```

Allocate a dictionary for the font. Leave room for the FID (fontID).

```
/FontType 3 def
```

FontType 3 indicates that this is a user defined font to the POSTSCRIPT font machinery.

```
/FontMatrix [1 0 0 1 0 0] def
/FontBBox [1.28 1.2 -0.16 -0.24] def
```

Use the identity matrix for the font coordinate system.
If all the characters in the font were overlapped, this would be the bounding box in the 1 unit character space.

```
/Encoding 256 array def
0 1 255 {Encoding exch /.notdef put} for
Encoding
dup 97 /a put   dup 105 /i put   dup 116 /t put
dup 98 /b put   dup 108 /l put   dup 117 /u put
dup 99 /c put   dup 109 /m put  dup 118 /v put
dup 100 /d put  dup 110 /n put  dup 119 /w put
dup 101 /e put  dup 111 /o put  dup 121 /y put
dup 102 /f put   dup 112 /p put  dup 32 /space put
dup 103 /g put  dup 114 /r put   dup 46 /period put
dup 104 /h put  dup 115 /s put   44 /comma put
```

Allocate space for the encoding vector.
Initialize all entries in the encoding vector with ''.notdef''.
Encode the lowercase letters and a few of the punctuation characters according to their ASCII encodings (decimal rather than octal codes have been used). Note that the lowercase letters j, k, q, x, and z are not encoded since we do not define character descriptions for them below (see ''CharData'' dictionary).

```
/BuildChar
  { 0 begin
    /char exch def
    /fontdict exch def
    /charname fontdict /Encoding get char get def

    /charinfo fontdict /CharData get charname
     get def
    /wx charinfo 0 get def
    /charbbox charinfo 1 4 getinterval def
    wx 0 charbbox aload pop setcachedevice

    charinfo 5 get charinfo 6 get true


    fontdict /imagemaskmatrix get
      dup 4 charinfo 7 get put
      dup 5 charinfo 8 get put
    charinfo 9 1 getinterval cvx
    imagemask
   end
  } def
```

The procedure ''BuildChar'' is called every time a character from this font must be constructed.
The character code and the font dictionary are provided as arguments to this procedure each time it's called.
Convert the character code to the corresponding name by looking it up in the encoding vector.
Now retrieve the data for printing that character in the ''CharData'' dictionary.
Find the width of that character.
Get the bounding box of the character.
Using the **setcachedevice** operator enables the characters from this font to be cached.
Get the width and height of the bitmap; set the invert boolean to **true** since the bitmaps specify the reverse image.
Insert the x and y translation components into the general **imagemask** matrix.

Get the hexadecimal string for printing the character in the form of an array, convert it into an executable object (procedure) and then print the bitmap image.

```
/BuildChar load 0 6 dict put
```

Create local storage for the procedure ''BuildChar.''

/imagemaskmatrix [25 0 0 -25 0 0] def

This is a template **imagemask** transformation matrix for this font. Since the bitmaps were designed to be 25 pixels from baseline to baseline and they are the same resolution in the x and y directions, both the x and y scale factors are 25. The y scale factor is negative because the bitmap images are specified beginning with the upper left corner rather than the lower left corner. (See description of the **imagemask** operator in the POSTSCRIPT Language Reference Manual.)

/CharData 25 dict def
CharData begin
/a [.64 .04 0 .56 .56 13 14 -1.5 13.5
    <0F983FD870786038C018C018C018C01
    8C018C018603870783FD80F98>] def
/b [.64 .04 0 .56 .76 13 19 -1.5 18.5
    <C000C000C000C000C000CF80DFE0F
    070E030C018C018C018C018C018C018
    E030F070DFE0CF80>] def
/c [.6 .04 0 .52 .56 12 14 -1.5 13.5
    <0F803FE070706030C000C000C000C00
    0C000C000603070703FE00F80>] def
/d [.64 .04 0 .56 .76 13 19 -1.5 18.5<001800180
    018001800180F983FD870786038C018C018
    C018C018C018C018603870783FD80F98>]def
/e [.64 .04 0 .56 .56 13 14 -1.5 13.5
    <0F803FE070706030C018C018FFF8FFF
    8C000C000603070703FE00F80>] def
/f [.32 0 0 .28 .76 7 19 -0.5 18.5 <0E1E3830
    30FEFE30303030303030303030303030>] def
/g [.64 .04 -0.16 .56 .56 13 18 -1.5 13.5<0F983F
    D870786038C018C018C018C018C018C018
    603870783FD80F98601870303FF00FC0>]def
/h [.6 .04 0 .52 .76 12 19 -1.5 18.5
    <C000C000C000C000C000CF80DFE0F070
    E030C030C030C030C030C030C030C030C
    030C030C030>] def
/i [.2 .04 0 .12 .76 2 19 -1.5 18.5 <C0C0C00000
    C0C0C0C0C0C0C0C0C0C0C0C0C0C0C0C0>] def
/l [.2 .04 0 .12 .76 2 19 -1.5 18.5<C0C0C0C0C0
    C0C0C0C0C0C0C0C0C0C0C0C0C0C0C0C0>] def
/m [.92 .04 0 .84 .56 20 14 -1.5 13.5
    <CF0780DFCFE0F0F870E07030C06030
    C06030C06030C06030C06030C06030
    C06030C06030C06030C06030>] def
/n [.6 .04 0 .52 .56 12 14 -1.5 13.5
    <CF80DFE0F070E030C030C030C030C0

The first number in the character description is the width of the character in the 1 unit font space. The next four numbers are the bounding box for the character in the 1 unit font space. The next two numbers are the width and height of the bitmap in pixels. The next two numbers are the x and y translation values for the transformation matrix provided to the **imagemask** operator. The last entry in the description is the hexadecimal string for printing the bitmap. (See below.)

Description of Data: Since the lowercase "i" is a relatively simple bitmap, it is used in this explanation. The bitmap for the "i" is 2 pixels (samples) wide and 19 pixels high. In order to print the bitmap, a hexadecimal string describing the pixel-image is provided as the contents of the procedure argument to the **imagemask** operator. Each pair of characters in the hexadecimal string description of the "i" represents a row of pixels; each row of the bitmap image should be padded out to the next byte boundary to ensure proper results. The matrix provided to the **imagemask** operator describes how to map the unit square in user space to the bitmap image space. The x and y translation components vary from character to character and indicate how many pixels to shift by so that the bitmap is positioned properly within user space. The y translation component will always be the height of the bitmap minus any displacement factor (such as for characters with descenders). The x component is usually the equivalent of the left sidebearing of the character in pixels. Note that both the x and y translation components have half a pixel (.5) subtracted from their original values. This is done to avoid round-off errors induced by trying to position the bitmap image right on a device pixel boundary.

```
     30C030C030C030C030C030C030> ] def
 /o [ .64 .04 0 .56 .56 13 14 -1.5 13.5
     <0F803FE070706030C018C018C018C0
     18C018C018603070703FE00F80> ] def
 /p [.64 .04 -.16 .56 .56 13 18 -1.5 13.5<CF80DF
     E0F070E030C018C018C018C018C018C018E
     030F070DFE0CF80C000C000C000C000>]def
 /r [ .32 .04 0 .28 .56 6 14 -1.5 13.5 <DCFCE0
     C0C0C0C0C0C0C0C0C0C0C0C0> ] def
 /s [ .36 0 0 .32 .56 8 14 -0.5 13.5
     <3C7EC3C3C0E0781E0703C3C37E3C> ] def
 /t [ .36 0 0 .32 .76 8 19 -0.5 18.5 <1818181818
     FFFF18181818181818181818181818> ] def
 /u [ .6 .04 0 .52 .56 12 14 -1.5 13.5
     <C030C030C030C030C030C030C030C0
     30C030C030C070E0F07FB01F30> ] def
 /v [ .48 0 0 .44 .56 11 14 -0.5 13.5
     <C060C060C06060C060C060C0318031
     8031801B001B001B000E000E00> ] def
 /w [ .88 0 0 .84 .56 21 14 -0.5 13.5
     <C07018C07018C0701860D83060D830
     60D830318C60318C60318C601B06C0
     1B06C01B06C00E03800E0380> ] def
 /y [.48 0 -.16 .44 .56 11 18 -.5 13.5<C060C060
     C06060C060C060C03180318031801B001B
     001F000600060006000C000C000C00>]def
 /period [.28 .08 0 .16 .12 2 3 -2.5 2.5
     <C0C0C0> ] def
 /comma [.32 0 -0.08 .2 .08 5 4 -0.5 1.5
     <183060C0> ] def
 /space [.24 0 0 0 0 1 1 0 0 <>] def
 /.notdef [.24 0 0 0 0 1 0 0 <>] def
  end
 /UniqueID 2 def
end
/Bitfont exch definefont pop
```

Pop the "CharData" dictionary.
Create a unique identifier for the font.
Done specifying the information required for the font.
Register the font and name it "Bitfont."

```
/Bitfont findfont 12 scalefont setfont
72 500 moveto (the tendency of the best) show
72 488 moveto (typography has been and) show
72 476 moveto (still should be in the path of) show
72 464 moveto (simplicity, legibility, and) show
72 452 moveto (orderly arrangement.) show
/Bitfont findfont 8 scalefont setfont
72 436 moveto (theodore low de vinne) show
showpage
```

The following lines illustrate the bitmap font in use.

Just like any other POSTSCRIPT font, the bitmap font can be scaled to any size.

FOR FURTHER REFERENCE

Adobe Systems, Inc. *POSTSCRIPT Language Reference Manual.* Addison-Wesley, Reading, Massachusetts, 1985.

Foley, James D. and Van Dam, Andries. *Fundamentals of Interactive Computer Graphics.* Addison-Wesley, Reading, Massachusetts, 1982.

IBM System/360: Priciples of Operation, Ninth Edition, November 1970.

Newman, William M. and Sproull, Robert F. *Principles of Interactive Computer Graphics.* McGraw-Hill, New York, 1979.

Pratt, Terrence W. *Programming Languages: Design and Implementation.* Prentice-Hall, Inc., Englewood Cliffs, N.J., 1975.

Warnock, John and Wyatt, Douglas. "A Device Independent Graphics Imaging Model for Use with Raster Devices," *Computer Graphics* Volume 16, Number 3, July 1982, pp. 313-320.

QUOTATIONS

page 174:   Daniel Berkeley Updike *Printing Types: Their History, Forms, & Use* Cambridge (Mass.) 1951, Vol. II, pp. 274-275.

page 152:   John C. Tarr *Design in Typography* London, 1951, p.21.

page 166:   Woody Allen Interview by *Time Magazine* April 30, 1979

page 206:   Valter Falk, Stockholm. *Manuale Typographicum* Frankfurt am Main 1954, p.34.

page 214:   William III from John Wesley, Journal June 6, 1765

page 214:   Napoleon I at Montereau February 17, 1814

page 214:   Abraham Lincoln Speech at Bloomington, Illinois May 19, 1856

page 214:   Victor Hugo in *France et Belgique - Alpes et Pyrenees - Voyages et Excursions* Paris 1910, pp. 215-216.

page 218:   Theodore Low De Vinne *A Treatise of Title Pages* New York 1902, p.439.

OPERATOR SUMMARY

Operand stack manipulation operators

any	**pop**	–	discard top element
$any_1\ any_2$	**exch**	$any_2\ any_1$	exchange top two elements
any	**dup**	any any	duplicate top element
$any_1..any_n\ n$	**copy**	$any_1..any_n\ any_1..any_n$	duplicate top n elements
$any_n..any_0\ n$	**index**	$any_n..any_0\ any_n$	duplicate arbitrary element
$a_{n-1}..a_0\ n\ j$	**roll**	$a_{(j-1)\ mod\ n}..a_0\ a_{n-1}..a_{j\ mod\ n}$	roll n elements up j times
$\vdash any_1..any_n$	**clear**	$\vdash$	discard all elements
$\vdash any_1..any_n$	**count**	$\vdash any_1..any_n\ n$	count elements on stack
–	**mark**	mark	push mark on stack
$mark\ obj_1..obj_n$	**cleartomark**	–	discard elements down through *mark*
$mark\ obj_1..obj_n$	**counttomark**	$mark\ obj_1..obj_n\ n$	count elements down to mark

Arithmetic and math operators

$num_1\ num_2$	**add**	sum	num_1 plus num_2
$num_1\ num_2$	**div**	quotient	num_1 divided by num_2
$int_1\ int_2$	**idiv**	quotient	integer divide
$int_1\ int_2$	**mod**	remainder	int_1 mod int_2
$num_1\ num_2$	**mul**	product	num_1 times num_2
$num_1\ num_2$	**sub**	difference	num_1 minus num_2
num_1	**abs**	num_2	absolute value of num_1
num_1	**neg**	num_2	negative of num_1
num_1	**ceiling**	num_2	ceiling of num_1
num_1	**floor**	num_2	floor of num_1
num_1	**round**	num_2	round num_1 to nearest integer
num_1	**truncate**	num_2	remove fractional part of num_1
num	**sqrt**	real	square root of *num*
num den	**atan**	angle	arctangent of *num*/*den* in degrees

angle	**cos**	real	cosine of *angle* (degrees)
angle	**sin**	real	sine of *angle* (degrees)
base exponent	**exp**	real	raise *base* to *exponent* power
num	**ln**	real	natural logarithm (base *e*)
num	**log**	real	logarithm (base 10)
–	**rand**	int	generate pseudo-random integer
int	**srand**	–	set random number seed
–	**rrand**	int	return random number seed

Array operators

int	**array**	array	create array of length *int*
–	**[**	mark	start array construction
mark $obj_0..obj_{n-1}$	**]**	array	end array construction
array	**length**	int	number of elements in *array*
array index	**get**	any	get array element indexed by *index*
array index any	**put**	–	put *any* into *array* at *index*
array index count	**getinterval**	subarray	subarray of *array* starting at *index* for *count* elements
$array_1$ index $array_2$	**putinterval**	–	replace subarray of $array_1$ starting at *index* by $array_2$
array	**aload**	$a_0..a_{n-1}$ array	push all elements of *array* on stack
$any_0..any_{n-1}$ array	**astore**	array	pop elements from stack into *array*
$array_1$ $array_2$	**copy**	$subarray_2$	copy elements of $array_1$ to initial subarray of $array_2$
array proc	**forall**	–	execute *proc* for each element of *array*

Packed Array operators

$any_0..any_{n-1}$ n	**packedarray**	packedarray	create packed array consisting of the specified *n* elements
–	**currentpacking**	bool	return array packing mode
bool	**setpacking**	–	set current array packing mode for '{...}' syntax (*true* = packedarray)
packedarray	**length**	int	number of elements in *packedarray*
packedarray index	**get**	any	get packedarray element indexed by *index*
packedarray index count	**getinterval**	subarray	subarray of *packedarray* starting at *index* for *count* elements
packedarray	**aload**	$a_0..a_{n-1}$ packedarray	push all elements of *packedarray* on stack
$packedarray_1$ $array_2$	**copy**	$subarray_2$	copy elements of $packedarray_1$ to initial subarray of $array_2$
packedarray proc	**forall**	–	execute *proc* for each element of *packedarray*

Dictionary operators

int	**dict**	dict	create dictionary with capacity for *int* elements
dict	**length**	int	number of key-value pairs in *dict*
dict	**maxlength**	int	capacity of *dict*

dict	**begin**	–	push *dict* on dict stack
–	**end**	–	pop dict stack
key value	**def**	–	associate *key* and *value* in current dict
key	**load**	value	search dict stack for *key* and return associated *value*
key value	**store**	–	replace topmost definition of *key*
dict key	**get**	any	get value associated with *key* in *dict*
dict key value	**put**	–	associate *key* with *value* in *dict*
dict key	**known**	bool	test whether *key* is in *dict*
key	**where**	dict true	
		or false	find dict in which *key* is defined
dict₁ dict₂	**copy**	dict₂	copy contents of *dict₁* to *dict₂*
dict proc	**forall**	–	execute *proc* for each element of *dict*
–	**errordict**	dict	push **errordict** on operand stack
–	**systemdict**	dict	push **systemdict** on operand stack
–	**userdict**	dict	push **userdict** on operand stack
–	**currentdict**	dict	push current dict on operand stack
–	**countdictstack**	int	count elements on dict stack
array	**dictstack**	subarray	copy dict stack into *array*

String operators

int	**string**	string	create string of length *int*
string	**length**	int	number of elements in *string*
string index	**get**	int	get string element indexed by *index*
string index int	**put**	–	put *int* into *string* at *index*
string index count	**getinterval**	substring	substring of *string* starting at *index* for *count* elements
string₁ index string₂	**putinterval**	–	replace substring of *string₁* starting at *index* by *string₂*
string₁ string₂	**copy**	substring₂	copy elements of *string₁* to initial substring of *string₂*
string proc	**forall**	–	execute *proc* for each element of *string*
string seek	**anchorsearch**	post match true	
		or string false	determine if *seek* is initial substring of *string*
string seek	**search**	post match pre true	
		or string false	search for *seek* in *string*
string	**token**	post token true	
		or false	read token from start of *string*

Relational, boolean, and bitwise operators

any₁ any₂	**eq**	bool	test equal
any₁ any₂	**ne**	bool	test not equal
num₁|str₁ num₂|str₂	**ge**	bool	test greater or equal
num₁|str₁ num₂|str₂	**gt**	bool	test greater than
num₁|str₁ num₂|str₂	**le**	bool	test less or equal
num₁|str₁ num₂|str₂	**lt**	bool	test less than
bool₁|int₁ bool₂|int₂	**and**	bool₃|int₃	logical | bitwise and

$bool_1$|int_1	**not**	$bool_2$|int_2		logical | bitwise not	

$bool_1$\|int_1 **not** $bool_2$\|int_2 — logical \| bitwise not
$bool_1$\|int_1 $bool_2$\|int_2 **or** $bool_3$\|int_3 — logical \| bitwise inclusive or
$bool_1$\|int_1 $bool_2$\|int_2 **xor** $bool_3$\|int_3 — logical \| bitwise exclusive or
— **true** true — push boolean value *true*
— **false** false — push boolean value *false*
int_1 shift **bitshift** int_2 — bitwise shift of int_1 (positive is left)

Control operators

any **exec** – execute arbitrary object
bool proc **if** – execute *proc* if *bool* is true
bool proc$_1$ proc$_2$ **ifelse** – execute *proc$_1$* if *bool* is true, *proc$_2$* if *bool* is false
init incr limit proc **for** – execute *proc* with values from *init* by steps of *incr* to *limit*
int proc **repeat** – execute *proc int* times
proc **loop** – execute *proc* an indefinite number of times
— **exit** – exit innermost active loop
— **stop** – terminate **stopped** context
any **stopped** bool establish context for catching **stop**
— **countexecstack** int count elements on exec stack
array **execstack** subarray copy exec stack into *array*
— **quit** – terminate interpreter
— **start** – executed at interpreter startup

Type, attribute, and conversion operators

any **type** name return name identifying *any*'s type
any **cvlit** any make object be literal
any **cvx** any make object be executable
any **xcheck** bool test executable attribute
array\|packedarray\|file\|string **executeonly** array\|packedarray\|file\|string reduce access to execute-only
array\|packedarray\|dict\|file\|string **noaccess** array\|packedarray\|dict\|file\|string disallow any access
array\|packedarray\|dict\|file\|string **readonly** array\|packedarray\|dict\|file\|string reduce access to read-only
array\|packedarray\|dict\|file\|string **rcheck** bool test read access
array\|packedarray\|dict\|file\|string **wcheck** bool test write access
num\|string **cvi** int convert to integer
string **cvn** name convert to name
num\|string **cvr** real convert to real
num radix string **cvrs** substring convert to string with radix
any string **cvs** substring convert to string

File operators

string$_1$ string$_2$ **file** file open file identified by *string$_1$* with access *string$_2$*
file **closefile** – close file

file	**read**	int true		read one character from *file*
		or false		
file int	**write**	–		write one character to *file*
file string	**readhexstring**	substring bool		read hex from *file* into *string*
file string	**writehexstring**	–		write *string* to *file* as hex
file string	**readstring**	substring bool		read string from *file*
file string	**writestring**	–		write characters of *string* to *file*
file string	**readline**	substring bool		read line from *file* into *string*
file	**token**	token true		
		or false		read token from *file*
file	**bytesavailable**	int		number of bytes available to read
–	**flush**	–		send buffered data to standard output file
file	**flushfile**	–		send buffered data or read to EOF
file	**resetfile**	–		discard buffered characters
file	**status**	bool		return status of *file*
string	**run**	–		execute contents of named file
–	**currentfile**	file		return file currently being executed
string	**print**	–		write characters of *string* to standard output file
any	**=**	–		write text representation of *any* to standard output file
⊢ any$_1$ .. any$_n$	**stack**	⊢ any$_1$ .. any$_n$		print stack nondestructively using =
any	**==**	–		write syntactic representation of *any* to standard output file
⊢ any$_1$ .. any$_n$	**pstack**	⊢ any$_1$ .. any$_n$		print stack nondestructively using ==
–	**prompt**	–		executed when ready for interactive input
bool	**echo**	–		turn on/off echoing

Virtual memory operators

–	**save**	save	create VM snapshot
save	**restore**	–	restore VM snapshot
–	**vmstatus**	level used maximum	report VM status

Miscellaneous operators

proc	**bind**	proc	replace operator names in *proc* by operators
–	**null**	null	push null on operand stack
–	**usertime**	int	return time in milliseconds
–	**version**	string	interpreter version

Graphics state operators

–	**gsave**	–	save graphics state
–	**grestore**	–	restore graphics state
–	**grestoreall**	–	restore to bottommost graphics state
–	**initgraphics**	–	reset graphics state parameters
num	**setlinewidth**	–	set line width
–	**currentlinewidth**	num	return current line width

int	**setlinecap**	–	set shape of line ends for stroke (0=butt, 1=round, 2=square)
–	**currentlinecap**	int	return current line cap
int	**setlinejoin**	–	set shape of corners for stroke (0=miter, 1=round, 2=bevel)
–	**currentlinejoin**	int	return current line join
num	**setmiterlimit**	–	set miter length limit
–	**currentmiterlimit**	num	return current miter limit
array offset	**setdash**	–	set dash pattern for stroking
–	**currentdash**	array offset	return current dash pattern
num	**setflat**	–	set flatness tolerance
–	**currentflat**	num	return current flatness
num	**setgray**	–	set color to gray value from 0 (black) to 1 (white)
–	**currentgray**	num	return current gray
hue sat brt	**sethsbcolor**	–	set color given hue, saturation, brightness
–	**currenthsbcolor**	hue sat brt	return current color hue, saturation, brightness
red green blue	**setrgbcolor**	–	set color given red, green, blue
–	**currentrgbcolor**	red green blue	return current color red, green, blue
freq angle proc	**setscreen**	–	set halftone screen
–	**currentscreen**	freq angle proc	return current halftone screen
proc	**settransfer**	–	set gray transfer function
–	**currenttransfer**	proc	return current transfer function

Coordinate system and matrix operators

–	**matrix**	matrix	create identity matrix
–	**initmatrix**	–	set CTM to device default
matrix	**identmatrix**	matrix	fill *matrix* with identity transform
matrix	**defaultmatrix**	matrix	fill *matrix* with device default matrix
matrix	**currentmatrix**	matrix	fill *matrix* with CTM
matrix	**setmatrix**	–	replace CTM by *matrix*
t_x t_y	**translate**	–	translate user space by (t_x, t_y)
t_x t_y matrix	**translate**	matrix	define translation by (t_x, t_y)
s_x s_y	**scale**	–	scale user space by s_x and s_y
s_x s_y matrix	**scale**	matrix	define scaling by s_x and s_y
angle	**rotate**	–	rotate user space by *angle* degrees
angle matrix	**rotate**	matrix	define rotation by *angle* degrees
matrix	**concat**	–	replace CTM by *matrix* × CTM
matrix$_1$ matrix$_2$ matrix$_3$	**concatmatrix**	matrix$_3$	fill *matrix$_3$* with *matrix$_1$* × *matrix$_2$*
x y	**transform**	x′ y′	transform (x, y) by CTM
x y matrix	**transform**	x′ y′	transform (x, y) by *matrix*
dx dy	**dtransform**	dx′ dy′	transform distance (dx, dy) by CTM
dx dy matrix	**dtransform**	dx′ dy′	transform distance (dx, dy) by *matrix*
x′ y′	**itransform**	x y	inverse transform (x′, y′) by CTM
x′ y′ matrix	**itransform**	x y	inverse transform (x′, y′) by *matrix*
dx′ dy′	**idtransform**	dx dy	inverse transform distance (dx′, dy′) by CTM

dx' dy' matrix	**idtransform** dx dy	inverse transform distance (dx', dy') by matrix
matrix$_1$ matrix$_2$	**invertmatrix** matrix$_2$	fill matrix$_2$ with inverse of matrix$_1$

Path construction operators

–	**newpath** –	initialize current path to be empty
–	**currentpoint** x y	return current point coordinate
x y	**moveto** –	set current point to (x, y)
dx dy	**rmoveto** –	relative moveto
x y	**lineto** –	append straight line to (x, y)
dx dy	**rlineto** –	relative lineto
x y r ang$_1$ ang$_2$	**arc** –	append counterclockwise arc
x y r ang$_1$ ang$_2$	**arcn** –	append clockwise arc
x$_1$ y$_1$ x$_2$ y$_2$ r	**arcto** xt$_1$ yt$_1$ xt$_2$ yt$_2$	append tangent arc
x$_1$ y$_1$ x$_2$ y$_2$ x$_3$ y$_3$	**curveto** –	append Bezier cubic section
dx$_1$ dy$_1$ dx$_2$ dy$_2$ dx$_3$ dy$_3$	**rcurveto** –	relative curveto
–	**closepath** –	connect subpath back to its starting point
–	**flattenpath** –	convert curves to sequences of straight lines
–	**reversepath** –	reverse direction of current path
–	**strokepath** –	compute outline of stroked path
string bool	**charpath** –	append character outline to current path
–	**clippath** –	set current path to clipping path
–	**pathbbox** ll$_x$ ll$_y$ ur$_x$ ur$_y$	return bounding box of current path
move line curve close	**pathforall** –	enumerate current path
–	**initclip** –	set clip path to device default
–	**clip** –	establish new clipping path
–	**eoclip** –	clip using even-odd inside rule

Painting operators

–	**erasepage** –	paint current page white
–	**fill** –	fill current path with current color
–	**eofill** –	fill using even-odd rule
–	**stroke** –	draw line along current path
width height bits/sample matrix proc	**image** –	render sampled image onto current page
width height invert matrix proc	**imagemask** –	render mask onto current page

Device setup and output operators

–	**showpage** –	output and reset current page
–	**copypage** –	output current page
matrix width height proc	**banddevice** –	install band buffer device
matrix width height proc	**framedevice** –	install frame buffer device
–	**nulldevice** –	install no-output device
proc	**renderbands** –	enumerate bands for output to device

Character and font operators

key font	**definefont**	font	register *font* as a font dictionary
key	**findfont**	font	return font dict identified by *key*
font scale	**scalefont**	font′	scale *font* by *scale* to produce new *font′*
font matrix	**makefont**	font′	transform *font* by *matrix* to produce new *font′*
font	**setfont**	–	set font dictionary
–	**currentfont**	font	return current font dictionary
string	**show**	–	print characters of *string* on page
$a_x\ a_y$ string	**ashow**	–	add (a_x, a_y) to width of each char while showing *string*
$c_x\ c_y$ char string	**widthshow**	–	add (c_x, c_y) to width of *char* while showing *string*
$c_x\ c_y$ char $a_x\ a_y$ string	**awidthshow**	–	combined effects of ashow and widthshow
proc string	**kshow**	–	execute *proc* between characters shown from *string*
string	**stringwidth**	$w_x\ w_y$	width of *string* in current font
–	**FontDirectory**	dict	dictionary of font dictionaries
–	**StandardEncoding**	array	standard font encoding vector

Font cache operators

–	**cachestatus**	bsize bmax msize mmax csize cmax blimit	
			return cache status and parameters
$w_x\ w_y\ ll_x\ ll_y\ ur_x\ ur_y$	**setcachedevice**	–	declare cached character metrics
$w_x\ w_y$	**setcharwidth**	–	declare uncached character metrics
num	**setcachelimit**	–	set max bytes in cached character
mark lower upper	**setcacheparams**	–	set character cache parameters
–	**currentcacheparams**	mark lower upper	
			return current font cache parameters

Errors

dictfull	no more room in dictionary
dictstackoverflow	too many begins
dictstackunderflow	too many ends
execstackoverflow	exec nesting too deep
handleerror	called to report error information
interrupt	external interrupt request (e.g., control-C)
invalidaccess	attempt to violate access attribute
invalidexit	exit not in loop
invalidfileaccess	unacceptable access string
invalidfont	invalid font name or dict
invalidrestore	improper restore
ioerror	input/output error occurred
limitcheck	implementation limit exceeded
nocurrentpoint	current point is undefined
rangecheck	operand out of bounds
stackoverflow	operand stack overflow

stackunderflow	operand stack underflow
syntaxerror	syntax error in POSTSCRIPT program text
timeout	time limit exceeded
typecheck	operand of wrong type
undefined	name not known
undefinedfilename	file not found
undefinedresult	over/underflow or meaningless result
unmatchedmark	expected mark not on stack
unregistered	internal error
VMerror	VM exhausted

Index

Colophon

Camera-ready copy for this book was created entirely with POSTSCRIPT and printed on a Linotronic 300 at Adobe Systems Incorporated. The book was created with the aid of the Scribe Document Production System (a product of UNILOGIC, Ltd.) as a Scribe document definition. The illustrations were POSTSCRIPT program segments which Scribe integrated and placed on the pages along with the formatted text portions.

Successive drafts of the book were processed with Scribe, each time generating a single POSTSCRIPT print file. The book was proofed when needed by printing the file on an Apple LaserWriter POSTSCRIPT printer. The final version was printed without modification on a Linotype Linotronic 300 typesetter and delivered to Addison-Wesley. No manual paste-up of any kind was required.

The typefaces used in this book were digitized by Adobe Systems Incorporated. The body type is Times Roman with Italic, Bold, and Bold Italic. The titles and examples are in Helvetica with Bold, Oblique, and Bold Oblique. The fixed width font used in some example output is Courier. Adobe's Symbol font is also featured.